Cook It

DK

LONDON, NEW YORK, MELBOURNE,
MUNICH, and DELHI

Senior designer Sonia Moore
Senior editor Carrie Love
Design Clare Marshall
Additional design Jane Ewart, Gemma Fletcher,
Ria Holland, Jessica Bentall, Claire Patane,
and Charlotte Bull
Additional editing Nikki Sims
US editor Margaret Parrish
Photographer Will Heap
Additional photography Dave King
Illustrator Takashi Mifune
Category publisher Mary Ling
Home economists Aya Nishimura,
Paul Jackman, and Kate Blinman
Picture researchers Romaine Werblow
Proofreader Jennifer Lane
Production editor Raymond Williams
Production controller Seyhan Esen
Hand model Max Moore

First American Edition, 2013
Published in the United States by
DK Publishing
375 Hudson Street
New York, New York 10014

13 14 15 16 10 9 8 7 6 5 4 3 2 1

001—187175—03/2013

Published in Great Britain by Dorling Kindersley Limited.

A catalog record for this book is available from the Library of Congress.

ISBN 978-1-4654-0254-7

DK books are available at special discounts when purchased in bulk
for sales promotions, premiums, fund-raising, or educational use. For
details, contact: DK Publishing Special Markets, 375 Hudson Street,
New York, New York 10014 or SpecialSales@dk.com.

Material used in this book was previously published in:
DK Children's Cookbook (2004)
Kids' Fun and Healthy Cookbook (2007)
Grow It, Cook It (2008)
The Children's Baking Book (2009)
The Ultimate Children's Cookbook (2010)
How Cooking Works (2012)

Color reproduction by Alta in London
Printed and bound by South China Ltd. in China

Discover more at
www.dk.com

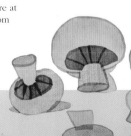

Contents

Introduction

Transforming a set of ingredients into something new is not only magical but is a great life skill. This book gives you ideas for trying new breakfasts, snacks, main meals, and sweet treats. Whether you want to fry an egg, bake cookies, or concoct something more complicated, such as jambalaya, just follow the easy steps in the recipes.

Key to Symbols used in the recipes

How many people the dish serves, or how many portions it makes

Preparation time, including chilling, freezing, and marinating

Cooking time
A few recipes, such as the salads, don't have this symbol.

Safety in the kitchen

Ask an adult to help when you see this symbol. Take extra care because hot ovens, stovetops, or sharp implements, such as knives, are involved.

Weights and measurements

Carefully measure or weigh ingredients before you start a recipe. Use measuring cups, scales, and a liquid measuring cup, as necessary. Below are the full names for measurements and their abbreviations.

Metric measures

g = gram

ml = milliliter

US measures

oz = ounce

lb = pound

Spoon measures

tsp = teaspoon

tbsp = tablespoon

Getting Started

1. Read a recipe all the way through before you begin.
2. Wash your hands, put on an apron, and tie back your hair.
3. Make sure you have all the ingredients and equipment before you begin a recipe.

Kitchen hygiene

When you're in the kitchen, follow these important rules to keep the germs in check.

• Always wash your hands before you start any recipe.

• Wash all fruits and vegetables.

• Use separate cutting boards for meat and vegetables.

• Keep your cooking area clean and have a cloth handy to wipe up any spills.

• Store raw and cooked food separately.

• Keep meat and fish in the fridge until you need them and always be sure to cook them properly.

• Wash your hands after handling raw eggs or raw meat.

• Always check the use-by date on all ingredients.

• Discard leftover marinade that has been used to soak meat in.

HEALTHY EATING

You need to eat a balanced diet made up of a variety of different foods so that you can grow, stay healthy, and have lots of energy for life.

Fruits and vegetables

Your body can get important vitamins and minerals, as well as fiber, from fruits and vegetables. Aim to eat about five different portions of these a day. It's useful to think of a portion as roughly equal to the amount you can hold in one hand—such as an apple, a small bunch of grapes, two broccoli florets, or a bowl of salad.

Starchy foods

Bread, cereals, rice, pasta, and potatoes are all starchy foods, also known as carbohydrates. These foods give you energy and should form a part of every meal—whether it's cereal for breakfast, a sandwich for lunch, or pasta for dinner. Many starchy foods come in whole wheat varieties, which are healthier for you because they contain more vitamins, minerals, and fiber when compared with the refined, white starches.

Protein

This type of food is made from amino acids, chemicals that work all over your body to keep you active and strong. We eat protein from both animal and plant sources—meat, fish, nuts and seeds, beans, and dairy produce. It's healthy to eat a variety of these.

Dairy produce

In addition to being a source of protein, dairy produce provides valuable vitamins (vitamins A, B12, and D) and minerals (such as calcium). Dairy produce includes milk, yogurt, cheese, butter, cream, crème fraiche, and cottage cheese. If you don't like the taste of dairy products, you can get these nutrients from other foods, such as soy milk, tofu, and baked beans.

Fats and sugars

Everyone needs fat for energy and for their bodies to work properly—but you need to eat the right type of fat. Fats also help you absorb vitamins and provide essential fatty acids, such as omega-3 and omega-6. Healthy fats (known as polyunsaturated or monounsaturated) are found in vegetable oils, such as sesame, sunflower, soy, and olive, as well as in nuts, seeds, avocados, and oily fish, such as mackerel and salmon. Avoid saturated and trans fats (found mostly in processed foods).

Sugary foods and salt

Sugar gives you energy and it makes cookies and cakes taste sweet. Eating too much sugar, though, can lead to mood swings, tooth decay, and obesity. Too much salt is linked with health problems. Avoid very salty snacks and don't add too much salt to your cooking.

Equipment

You need to use the right equipment for each step. Most kitchens are equipped with the majority of these tools. Remember to be extra careful when using equipment that is sharp or requires electricity to power it. An adult should always supervise you while you're in the kitchen.

Whisk

Kitchen scissors

Pizza cutter

Fork

Peelers

Garlic crusher

Wooden Spoons

Basting brush

Large Spoon

Sharp knife

Table knife

Spoons

Grater

Baking pans

Loaf pan

Nonstick muffin pan

Pizza pan

Plastic cutting boards

Cooling rack

Plastic container

Small bowls

Large bowl

Colander

Glass bowls

Milk pan

Wok

Food processor

Cutting board

Piping bag

Glass jar

Potato masher

Electric mixer

Blender

Spatula

Plastic spatula

Ladle

Skewers

Measuring Spoons

Strainer

Egg cup

Slotted Spoon

Spaghetti claw

Ice cream Scoop

Liquid measuring cup

Pastry cutter

Ramekin

Juicer

Cookie cutters

Springform cake pan

Pitchers

Rolling pin

Parchment paper

Square cake pan

Foil

Oven dish

Ceramic pie dish

Lasagne dish

Metal pie pan

Plastic wrap

Stock pot

Frying pan

Small casserole dish

Saucepan with lid

Grill pan

Ways to cook

Some foods are best cooked on low heat for a long time, while others respond best to a fast blast of heat. The techniques shown below are used in different recipes to bring out the best flavors and textures of each dish.

Boil

With the heat turned up high, a liquid will bubble vigorously when boiling.

Simmer

With the heat on low, a mixture will bubble gently when simmering.

Fry

Drizzle oil into a wide pan to fry food; frying is also called sautéing.

Stir-fry

On high heat and using oil, stir-frying cooks food fast and requires lots of stirring.

Broil

With the heat coming from above, food needs to be turned during broiling.

Grill

On high heat, a grill pan's ridges leave smoky stripes on the food.

Bake

Cooking food in an oven is baking. Bread, cookies, cakes, and pies are baked.

Roast

Cooking meat, fish, or vegetables in the oven is known as roasting.

Steam

Food is placed above boiling water and steam is used to cook it.

Poach

Cooking in a simmering liquid, such as water or milk, is called poaching.

Deep-fry

Completely immersing food in hot oil is known as deep-frying.

BBQ

Food can be grilled on a BBQ using heat from charcoal.

Preparing ingredients

Before you start cooking you'll need to get all your ingredients ready. Depending on your recipe, you may have a lot of prep work to do or very little.

Dice

To dice an onion, first slice it (while keeping it together) and then slice it at right angles to create small squares, dice, or cubes. For zucchini, first cut into chunky sticks and then cut across these.

Chop

Claw Hold the food using a "claw" shape to keep fingers clear of the knife.

Bridge Form a bridge between thumb and finger and cut beneath the bridge.

Peel

Whatever you're peeling, hold the food in one hand and peel away from your body. Carrots are easily peeled from top to bottom, but apples can be peeled in one beautiful spiral—with practice. Watch out for your fingers—peelers are sharp!

Grate

As the food passes over the grater's teeth, slithers are forced through.

Mash

Cooked root vegetables can be pushed through a masher until smooth.

Before

After

Make bread crumbs

It's quickest done in a food processor. Tear pieces of dried bread into the bowl, put the lid on, and process until crumbed. Or, you can grate chunks of the bread instead.

Other useful terms

- **Toast** to make a food, such as bread or nuts, crisp, hot, and brown (see page 81)
- **Purée** to blend vegetable or fruit pulp until smooth in a food processor or blender or by pushing it through a strainer (see page 31)
- **Marinate** to mix food with a combination of oil, wine, or vinegar with herbs or spices to add flavor (see page 76, 77, 88–89)

- **Blend** to mix together so you can't see any of the individual ingredients (see page 112)
- **Punch down** to knock excess air out of bread dough after it has risen (see page 41)
- **Drizzle** to pour a little stream of liquid, such as olive oil, in tiny drops (see page 81)
- **Season** to add salt and pepper

- **Toss** to mix dry ingredients in wet ingredients, such as lettuce leaves in salad dressing or pasta shapes in a sauce (see page 57)
- **Reduce to thicken** to heat a sauce gently until some of its water is lost (as steam) and the amount of sauce becomes less (see page 83)
- **Baste** to coat food with meat juice, a marinade, or butter while cooking (see page 93)

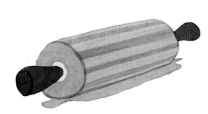

Ways to bake

If you want your cakes to rise, make light meringue, or perfect your pastries and cookies, there are certain baking techniques you will need to master. Once you know what's what, you'll be a baking expert!

Sift

Sift confectioners' sugar or flour through a strainer to remove lumps and add air.

Fold

1. Use a spatula to mix gently while keeping the air in the mixture.

2. Go around the edge of the bowl and then "cut" across, lifting as you go.

Beat

Make a smooth, airy mixture by working fast with a wooden spoon.

Separate an egg

1. Break the shell: tap the egg on the side of the bowl and open up.

2. Transfer the yolk from one shell to the other; put the yolk in another bowl.

Whisk egg whites

1. Mix a lot of air into a mixture using an electric mixer or handheld whisk.

2. The mixture should be stiff; if you overbeat it, the mixture will collapse.

Rub in

1. Many recipes mix fat (diced butter) and flour using this method.

2. Using your fingertips, pick up the mixture, break up the lumps, and let it fall.

3. Keep rubbing your thumb along your fingertips. To check that you've gotten rid of any butter lumps, shake the bowl and the lumps will pop up to the surface.

Make a piping bag

1. Cut a square of wax paper or parchment paper.
2. Fold the paper around on itself to form a cone with a pointed end. Tape in place.

3. Snip off the end of the cone for the icing or frosting to come out: for a fine line, use a tiny cut; cut higher up the cone for a thicker line.

Cream

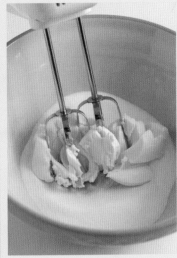

1. When mixing butter and sugar together, use butter that's been left to soften at room temperature.
2. Cut the butter into pieces.

3. Using an electric mixer or a wooden spoon, beat the butter and sugar together until the mixture is pale in color and light and fluffy.

Knead

1. Use the heel of your hand to push the bread dough away from you.

2. Fold the squashed end of dough over and turn all the dough around.

3. Repeat the squashing, folding, and turning motions until the dough is silky soft and smooth. Now the dough is ready to prove (see page 40).

Roll out

On a floured surface, push down on a rolling pin to make a large flat piece.

Grease a pan

Use parchment paper to spread a thin layer of butter over the pan.

Line a pan

1. Draw around your pan and add some extra for the paper to go up the sides.

2. Position the paper in the pan. Fold at the corners; snip off excess.

BREAKFAST BITES

Ingredients

- 4 large eggs
- 1 cup milk
- 1/4 tsp ground cinnamon
- 4 slices thick white bread, cut into triangles
- 2 tbsp vegetable oil
- 2/3 cup blueberries
- maple syrup, to serve

Equipment

- whisk
- mixing bowl
- shallow dish
- frying pan and spatula

French toast

Popular around the world, this dish is eaten in Portugal at Christmas and in Spain and Brazil at Easter.

Serves 2   10 mins   10 mins

1

Crack the eggs into a mixing bowl. Add the milk and cinnamon and whisk together.

2

Pour the mixture into a shallow dish. Soak the bread for about 30 seconds in the mixture.

3

Heat half a tablespoon of the oil in a frying pan on low heat. Carefully place two triangles in the pan.

4

Fry the triangles on both sides until they turn golden brown. Repeat steps 3 and 4 for the remaining bread triangles.

5

Serve the French toast warm with blueberries and maple syrup, or try it with butter and jam.

Four ways with eggs

Try these classic ways to cook an egg.

Boiled eggs

Boiled eggs are easy to make. How do you like your boiled egg? You can have it soft-, medium-, or hard-boiled.

Ingredients

This recipe is for 1 person. It takes 2 minutes to prepare and 4-8 minutes to cook.

• 1 egg

• 1 slice buttered toast, to serve

Method

• Fill a saucepan with water and use a slotted spoon to lower 1 egg into it. Ask an adult to boil the water.

• Once the water has boiled, lower the temperature and simmer. Follow these cooking times:

soft-boiled = 4 minutes
medium-boiled = 6 minutes
hard-boiled = 8 minutes

• Once the egg is cooked, use a slotted spoon to remove it from the pan. Place in an egg cup. Tap the top with the back of a teaspoon. Carefully slice off the top with the spoon. Serve with buttered toast.

Scrambled eggs

Scrambled eggs are delicious on their own or as part of a cooked breakfast. You can add different ingredients, such as bacon.

Ingredients

This recipe is for 1 person. It takes 2 minutes to prepare and 8 minutes to cook.

• 1 slice bacon

• 1 tbsp milk

• 1 egg

• a small pat of butter

• 1 slice buttered toast, to serve

• dried basil, to serve

Method

• Ask an adult to fry the bacon. When it's cooked, use a knife and fork to cut it up into small pieces.

• In a small glass bowl, use a whisk to mix the milk and egg together until creamy.

• Melt the butter in a small frying pan over medium heat and add the egg and milk mixture. Stir often until the eggs are just cooked, but still creamy. Stir in the bacon pieces with a wooden spoon.

• Sprinkle the dried basil over the eggs and serve on toast.

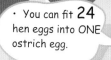

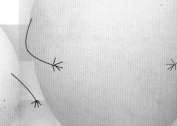

· You can fit **24** hen eggs into ONE ostrich egg.

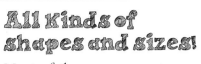

All kinds of shapes and sizes!

Most of the eggs we eat come from hens, but you can buy lots of different types. Go ahead and eggs-periment!

Quail · Duck · Hen · Gull · Goose · Ostrich

 3

4

Poached egg

Poaching is a fun and satisfying way to cook an egg. You'll need an adult to help you because poached eggs can be tricky to make.

Ingredients

This recipe is for 1 person. It takes 1 minute to prepare and 1–2 minutes to cook.

· 1 egg; use a really fresh egg for the best results

· 1 white English muffin, halved, toasted, and buttered, to serve

Method

● Fill a wide, shallow pan with water and ask an adult to heat it on the stovetop.

● When the water is simmering, use the handle of a slotted spoon to swirl the water around to make a whirlpool.

● Crack the egg into a small cup and tip into the center of the whirlpool.

● To give the cooked egg a round shape, use a spoon to keep the water moving gently while cooking.

● When the egg is done, use a slotted spoon to remove it from the pan. Drain on paper towels. Season with black pepper. Serve with the English muffin.

Fried egg

Fried eggs are quick to make and make a filling breakfast. They are best served in a roll or on toast.

Ingredients

This recipe is for 1 person. It takes 1 minute to prepare and 2–4 minutes to cook.

· 1 tsp sunflower oil

· 1 egg

· 1 bread roll, halved and buttered, to serve

Method

● Ask an adult to heat the oil in a pan over medium heat.

● Crack the egg into a bowl. If any of the shell falls into the bowl, scoop it out using a spoon. Gently pour the egg into the frying pan.

● The egg needs to be fried for about two minutes on medium heat. If you like your egg well-done, it needs to be cooked on both sides.

● Serve the fried egg on a buttered bread roll. Season with freshly ground pepper.

15

Ingredients

- 2 tbsp sunflower or vegetable oil
- 6 tbsp corn syrup or honey
- 2¼ cups oats
- 4oz (115g) hazelnuts
- ¼ cup pumpkin seeds
- 4oz (115g) dried banana chips, broken into small pieces
- ¾ cup raisins
- natural or plain yogurt to serve

Equipment

- large saucepan
- wooden spoon
- large bowl
- baking sheet
- oven mitts
- airtight container for storing cereal

Fruity cereal

You need a hearty breakfast to keep you going through the morning. This delicious cereal will keep you filled up until snack time. You can try using dried cranberries instead of raisins.

Ask an adult to preheat the oven to 400°F (200°C). Heat the oil and corn syrup (or honey) in a saucepan over low heat.

Pour the corn syrup and oil mixture into a large bowl with the oats, hazelnuts, and pumpkin seeds.

Place the mixture onto a baking sheet, spread it out, and cook it in the oven for 10 minutes, or until the cereal turns golden brown.

Let the oat mixture cool down on the tray and then pour it into a bowl. Add the dried banana chips and raisins to the mixture and stir well.

Serves 8   5 mins   20 mins

Storage

Store your cereal in an airtight container and have it for breakfast several times over the next few weeks. Don't eat it all yourself! Let your family and friends try some, too.

5

Serve your cereal in a bowl with milk or a spoonful of plain yogurt. ⚠

Fruit smoothies

Smoothies are lots of fun to make and drink. You can create many variations by using different fruits or by adding oats to make your drink a bit thicker.

Here are three recipes...

3 Serves   7 mins

Banana and mango smoothie

Ingredients

- ¾ cup milk,
- ½ cup plain yogurt,
- 2 small bananas, sliced,
- 1 small mango, peeled and coarsely chopped

Equipment

- Cutting board, sharp knife, blender, glasses for smoothies

Method

- Follow the steps for the blueberry smoothie.

Blueberry, orange, and strawberry smoothie

Ingredients

- ½ cup pulp-free orange juice
- ½ cup milk
- ½ cup plain yogurt
- 1 cup blueberries
- 6oz (150g) strawberries, hulled
- 3 tbsp oats
- ½ tsp pure vanilla extract (optional)

Equipment

- Cutting board, sharp knife, blender, glasses for smoothies

Method

- Put all the ingredients into a blender and run it on medium to high speed until everything is well mixed and smooth.
- Pour the smoothie into three glasses and serve it to your family or friends.
- Drink right away, or you'll need to stir your smoothie because it will thicken and separate.

Peach and berry smoothie

Ingredients

- ½ cup milk,
- ½ cup plain yogurt
- 2 peaches, sliced
- 3 oz (75g) raspberries,
- 3 oz (75g) strawberries, hulled
- 1 tbsp oats

Equipment

- Cutting board, sharp knife, blender, glasses for smoothies

Method

- Follow the steps for the Blueberry, orange, and strawberry smoothie.

19

Sticky Stuff

The sugar and corn syrup act like glue in this recipe. They help the dry ingredients to stick together, making the granola bars incredibly chewy and sticky!

Fruit bars

Granola bars are perfect for breakfast or as a snack. Once you've mastered this recipe, experiment with other fruits and nuts.

Serves 12   15 mins   30 mins

Ingredients

- 8 tbsp unsalted butter
- ½ cup light brown sugar, packed
- ½ cup corn syrup or honey
- 2 cups oats
- ¾ cup raisins
- 2oz (50g) mixed nuts, chopped

Equipment

- 12 x 9 x 1½in (30 x 23 x 4cm) baking pan
- parchment paper
- wooden spoon
- saucepan

1

Ask an adult to preheat the oven to 300°F (150°C). Grease your baking pan, then line it with 2 sheets of parchment paper.

2

Ask an adult to melt the butter, sugar, and corn syrup (or honey) in a saucepan over low heat.

3

Place all the other ingredients in a large bowl and pour in the sugar mixture.

4

Spread the mixture evenly in the baking pan. Press down firmly to make sure the mixture holds together. Bake for 20–30 minutes, or until golden brown.

5

When the granola bars are baked, let them cool for 5 minutes and then cut them into 12 squares. Hold the warm pan with a cloth. Take the squares out when they're cool and firm.

LIGHT BITES

Tomato and couscous salad

Serves 4   30 mins

Salad makes a great light lunch or it can be eaten as an appetizer. This super salad is full of interesting ingredients and looks pretty on the plate. It's tasty, too!

Ingredients

- 4 large tomatoes
- 2/3 cup tomato juice
- 3/4 cup couscous
- 2oz (50g) golden raisins
- handful of basil leaves, chopped
- handful of flat-leaf parsley, torn (optional)
- freshly ground black pepper

Equipment

- sharp knife
- cutting board
- teaspoon
- small glass bowl
- large glass bowl
- fork
- tablespoon

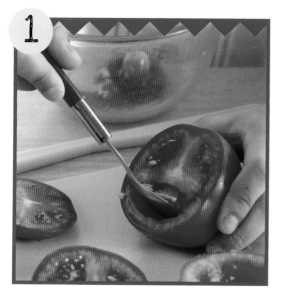

1

Slice the tops off the tomatoes and scoop out the insides. Put the seeds and flesh into a bowl with the tomato juice.

2

Pour ½ cup hot water over the couscous and let it stand for 10 minutes. Fluff up the grains. Add the tomato mixture.

3

Add the golden raisins, basil, and parsley (if using), and mix. Taste, and season with freshly ground pepper.

4

Spoon the mixture into the tomato shells. Serve with any leftover couscous mixture and garnish with crisp lettuce.

23

Tuna and bean salad

Salads are good for you because they help you get the five portions of fruits and vegetables you need each day. This salad combines wonderful flavors and is fun to make.

Ingredients

- ½ cup frozen fava beans
- 3 x 5oz (140g) cans tuna in olive oil, drained
- 10 cherry tomatoes, halved
- handful of fresh chives, finely chopped
- freshly ground black pepper
- 12 black olives, pitted
- 1 crisp head of lettuce, such as cos, leaves separated
- 2-3 scallions, finely sliced

For the dressing

- 6 tbsp extra virgin olive oil
- 1 garlic clove, finely chopped
- 2 tbsp lemon juice
- 1-2 tsp Dijon mustard

Equipment

- large glass bowl
- colander
- screw-top jar
- 4 serving bowls

1

Soak the fava beans in hot water for five minutes, then use a colander to drain them. Set the beans aside.

2

To make the dressing, put all the ingredients in a screw-top jar, season with pepper, screw the lid on tightly, and shake!

3

Place the tuna, tomatoes, and half of the dressing in a bowl. Sprinkle in half the chives and season with pepper. Gently mix in the beans and olives.

4

Spoon the tuna mixture on top of the lettuce leaves. Drizzle the remaining dressing over the top. Sprinkle in the scallions and remaining chives.

Extras

If you don't like tuna
then you can substitute
15oz (425g) of cooked ham
slices or cooked chicken
pieces, shredded. Also, green
olives work just as well as
black olives.

Picnic salad

Ingredients

- 1¼ cups couscous
- 1¼ cups hot vegetable stock
- ½ cucumber
- 1 medium-sized pomegranate (if you like, use packages of prepeeled fruit to save on prep time)
- 2 tbsp olive oil
- 8oz (250g) cherry tomatoes
- grated zest and juice of 1 lemon
- 1 small red onion, thinly sliced
- 7oz (200g) feta cheese, crumbled
- 1 large bunch mint, freshly chopped (about 6 tbsp)

Equipment

- 3 bowls
- liquid measuring cup
- fork
- cutting board
- knife
- teaspoon
- wooden spoon

This is another delicious salad. You can substitute any of your favorite cheeses—such as Cheddar, mozzarella, or Brie—for the feta cheese and add other ingredients, like olives, peppers, and scallions.

Place the couscous in a large bowl and pour in the hot stock. Let stand for 5 minutes, until all the liquid has been absorbed. Allow to cool.

Cut the cherry tomatoes in half. Halve the cucumber lengthwise and scoop out the seeds with a teaspoon, then chop into small pieces.

Cut the pomegranate in half and hold one half over a bowl. Lightly tap the pomegranate with a wooden spoon, until the seeds fall into the bowl.

Add the lemon juice, lemon zest, and olive oil to the couscous. Stir in the tomatoes, cucumber, red onion, feta cheese, mint, and pomegranate seeds.

Serves 4   15 mins   20 mins

Tomato soup

Soup can be served as a healthy snack or as an appetizer to a main meal. This recipe makes a thick and creamy soup that's topped with small pieces of toast, called croutons.

Serves 2-4   20 mins   35 mins

Ingredients

- 1 small onion
- 1 small carrot
- 2 tbsp olive oil
- 1 garlic clove, crushed
- 1 tbsp all-purpose flour
- 14.5oz (400g) can chopped tomatoes

- 1 tbsp tomato paste
- 1 tsp fresh thyme leaves, optional
- 2 cups vegetable stock
- freshly ground black pepper
- 1 pinch granulated sugar
- 1 squeeze lemon juice

- 2 thick slices white bread
- 2 tbsp olive oil
- salt and freshly ground black pepper

Equipment

- sharp knife
- vegetable peeler
- cutting board

- medium saucepan
- wooden spatula
- bread knife
- nonstick baking sheet
- oven mitts
- ladle
- blender

1

Preheat the oven to 425°F (220°C). Peel and chop the onion and carrot. Heat the oil in the saucepan over medium heat.

2

Add the onion and carrot and cook for about 5 minutes to soften, stirring occasionally. Stir in the garlic and flour and cook the mixture for 1 minute.

3

Add the tomatoes, tomato paste, thyme, stock, sugar, and lemon juice to the pan and bring to a boil. Reduce the heat and simmer for 20–25 minutes.

4

Meanwhile, cut the bread into 1in (2cm) cubes. Scatter the bread onto the baking sheet and drizzle olive oil over the top. Season with salt and pepper.

5

Use your hands to coat the bread in the oil. Bake for 8–10 minutes, until crisp and golden. Shake the baking sheet every few minutes for even cooking.

6

Carefully ladle the hot soup into the blender. Season the soup with pepper, and blend until smooth. Ladle the soup into bowls and serve.

Ingredients

- 2¼lb (1 kg) butternut squash
- salt
- freshly ground black pepper
- 1 tbsp vegetable oil
- 1 onion, chopped
- 2½ cups hot vegetable stock
- 2 tbsp honey

To serve
- baguette
- Gruyére or Swiss cheese

Equipment

- tablespoon
- vegetable peeler
- baking sheet
- wooden spoon
- food processor
- large saucepan

Butternut squash soup

This wholesome, warming soup is perfect for a cold day. It's made from roasted butternut squash, but you can also make the soup with pumpkin, if you like.

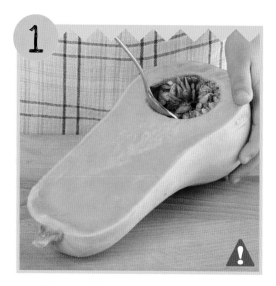

Preheat the oven to 400°F (200°C). Cut the butternut squash in half lengthwise. Using a spoon, scoop out the seeds and pith.

Cut into large chunks. Use a vegetable peeler to remove the peel. Cut the chunks into 1in (2.5cm) cubes.

Place on a baking sheet, season with salt and pepper, and drizzle the oil over the top. Roast for 20 minutes. Remove from the oven.

Add the onion and stir. Return to the oven and cook for another 15 minutes.

Place the butternut squash and onion in a food processor with half of the stock. Blend until smooth.

6

Place the purée in a saucepan with the remaining stock and honey. Simmer for 3 to 4 minutes. Serve with slices of toasted baguette, cheese, and parsley.

Serves 4   15 mins   39 mins

Basic bread

This recipe is so simple and enjoyable to make. Use the dough for a traditional loaf of bread or bake delicious rolls instead. The recipe makes eight rolls.

Bread rolls

At Step 5, divide the dough into 8 balls, place them on a greased baking sheet and flatten them slightly. Cover with a damp dish towel, and let rise for 30 minutes. Brush the tops with milk. Bake for 20 minutes.

Ingredients

- 1½ tsp active dry yeast
- 1 tsp sugar
- 1½ cups lukewarm water
- 3⅔ cups white bread flour
- 2 tsp salt

Equipment

- 2lb loaf pan
- strainer
- mixing bowl
- plastic wrap
- cooling rack

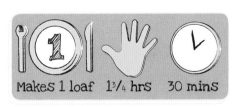

Makes 1 loaf   1¾ hrs   30 mins

1

Lightly grease the loaf pan with butter. Place the yeast, sugar, and a little of the water in a small bowl. Stir well and let stand in a warm place for 10 minutes, until frothy.

2

Sift the flour and salt into a large mixing bowl. Make a well in the center and pour in the yeast mixture and remaining water. Stir to form a dough. Knead the dough for 10 minutes on a floured surface.

3

Place the dough back in the bowl, cover with a damp dish towel, and let stand in a warm place for an hour. Punch down the dough to knock out the large air bubbles.

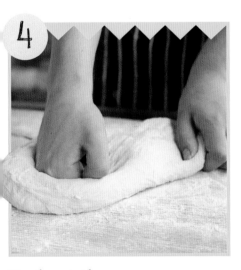

4

Preheat the oven to 425°F (220°C). Knead the dough gently on a lightly floured surface.

5

It will DOUBLE in size!

Shape the dough into a rectangle, tuck the ends under, and place in the pan. Cover with the damp dish towel and let rise in a warm place for another 30 minutes.

6

Place the pan in the center of the oven. Bake for 30 minutes, or until risen and golden. Turn out the loaf and tap the bottom—it should sound hollow. Place it on a cooling rack.

Italian bread

Ingredients

- 2½ cups white bread flour
- ¼oz envelope active dry yeast
- ½ tsp salt
- ¾ cup warm water
- ¼ cup, plus 1 tbsp olive oil
- 6 cherry tomatoes, halved
- 6 black olives, sliced
- sea salt, for sprinkling

Equipment

- strainer
- large mixing bowl
- large metal spoon
- baking sheet
- clean, damp dish towel

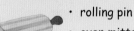 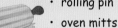

- rolling pin
- oven mitts

This dimpled bread is known as focaccia and can be flavored with herbs, cheese, sun-dried tomatoes, or olives. It's so yummy, you'll keep coming back for more!

1

Sift the flour into a large mixing bowl, add the salt, and stir in the yeast with a large metal spoon. Lightly oil a baking sheet to prevent the focaccia from sticking.

2

Make a well in the center of the flour with the large metal spoon. Stir in the warm water and olive oil until the mixture starts to come together to form a smooth dough.

3

Transfer to a floured surface and knead for 10 minutes, until smooth and elastic. Place in the bowl, cover with a damp dish towel, and let rise in a warm place for 1 hour.

4

Punch down the dough to remove the large air bubbles, then place on a floured surface. Roll out to an 8in (20cm) circle about ½in (1cm) thick.

5

Place the rolled-out dough on the oiled baking sheet and cover with a clean, damp dish towel. Let the dough rise in a warm place for 30 minutes.

Preheat the oven to 400°F

(200°C). Using your fingertips, make dimples all over the surface of the risen dough.

Drizzle with olive oil and

place rosemary in a third of the dimples. Fill the middle third with the tomatoes and olives, and sprinkle sea salt over the final third.

Place in the oven on the

middle rack. Bake for 20–25 minutes, until risen and golden brown. Delicious eaten warm!

Sunflower loaves

Fill your kitchen with the homey smell of bread-making. Sunflower seeds are great to nibble on, too, while your bread is baking.

Ingredients

- 2 cups white bread flour
- 1 cup whole wheat flour
- 1 tsp salt
- 1 tsp granulated sugar
- ¹⁄₄oz (7g) envelope dry-active yeast
- 1 cup warm water
- 2 tbsp extra virgin olive oil, plus extra for oiling pots
- ³⁄₄ cup sunflower seeds
- a little milk

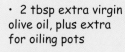

Equipment

- 4 terra-cotta flower pots, 5in x 4in (11cm x 10cm)
- liquid measuring cup
- mixing bowl
- baking sheet
- plastic bag
- pastry brush
- wooden spoon

Scrub the pots with clean water. Ask an adult to preheat the oven to 400°F (200°C). Oil the pots inside and out and bake for 35–40 minutes. Let them cool. Repeat this process twice more.

Put the flour, salt, sugar, and yeast into a large bowl. Make a well in the center and pour in the water and olive oil. Mix to make a soft, but firm dough.

Turn the dough out onto a lightly dusted work surface and knead well for at least 10 minutes (use a timer). Ask an adult to take a turn if your arms get tired.

Make a dip in the dough and add three-quarters of the sunflower seeds. Knead them into the dough so that they're spread evenly throughout.

Divide the dough into four pieces and place one ball into each flower pot. Cover the pots with a plastic bag and leave until the dough has doubled in size.

Brush the tops of the risen loaves with a little milk. Sprinkle the remaining sunflower seeds on top and bake for 35–40 minutes, or until golden. Cool in the pots.

Cornbread

Ingredients

- 1 cup all-purpose flour
- 1 cup cornmeal or polenta
- 1 tbsp baking powder
- 1 tsp salt
- 5 scallions, thinly chopped (optional)
- 1 cup canned corn
- 2 medium eggs
- 1 ¼ cups buttermilk or natural yogurt
- ½ cup milk
- 4 tbsp butter, melted and cooled

Equipment

- 8in (20cm) square cake pan or 8in (20cm) round ceramic pie dish
- large mixing bowl
- wooden spoon
- liquid measuring cup
- small hand whisk
- oven mitts
- sharp knife

This cornbread recipe is really simple to make and the corn and scallions give it an unusual chunky texture to the light dough.

Grease an 8in (20cm) square cake pan or a round 8in (20cm) ceramic pie dish. The recipe works in either a pan or a dish. Preheat the oven to 400°F (200°C).

In a large mixing bowl, pour in the flour, cornmeal or polenta, baking powder, salt, chopped scallions, and corn. Mix together thoroughly with a wooden spoon and set aside.

In a liquid measuring cup, whisk together the eggs, buttermilk (or yogurt), milk, and melted butter with a small whisk until they are well combined and frothy.

Pour the egg and milk mixture into the flour mixture in the large mixing bowl. Stir with a wooden spoon to combine all the ingredients thoroughly.

Makes 12   10 mins   30 mins

5

Pour the mixture into the prepared pan. Bake for 25–30 minutes, until golden brown and beginning to pull away from the sides of the pan. Allow to cool in the pan before cutting into wedges.

Pizza dough

Pizza is a popular meal to eat for lunch or dinner. It's easy to learn how to make the dough for the crust. This recipe makes enough dough for four pizzas.

Ingredients

- 3²/₃ cups white bread flour
- ¼oz envelope active dry yeast
- a pinch of salt
- 1 cup warm water
- ¼ cup olive oil

Equipment

- strainer
- large glass bowl
- wooden spoon
- plastic wrap
- baking sheet or pan
- rolling pin

makes 4 pizzas · 1 hr

Sift the flour into a bowl and add the yeast and salt. Make a well in the center, then slowly add the warm water.

Mix with a wooden spoon until all ingredients come together. Add the olive oil and continue to mix until you have a soft dough.

Knead firmly using the heel of your hand, folding the dough over as you go. Do this until the dough becomes soft and spongy.

Put the dough in a bowl, cover with plastic wrap, and let stand n a warm place for 30–40 minutes, or until the dough has doubled in size.

Pull the dough out on a floured surface, and knead with your knuckles to punch down the air. Fold the dough over and knead again.

It will become elastic and stretchy

6 **Divide the dough** into four balls. Roll each ball out onto a floured surface until it is about ½in (1cm) thick. Place on a pizza pan or in a metal pan. You can try different toppings.

The dough pictured is topped with 3 tbsp tomato paste, 3 sliced tomatoes, and 6oz (150g) mozarella, torn into pieces, and fresh basil leaves.

Bake for 15–20 minutes, or until the crust is golden and the cheese is bubbling.

Four ways with pizzas

Try out these classic and new pizzas.

1

Tiny tomatoes pizza

This is a classic combination of ingredients and flavors. Restaurants that serve pizza would have this at the top of their menus.

Ingredients

• pizza dough ball (from the recipe on pages 40–41)

• 2–3 tbsp tomato paste

• large mozzarella ball

• 1 container plum or cherry tomatoes

• fresh basil leaves, to serve

Method

• Roll out the pizza dough on a floured surface into a circle that will fit your pizza pan.

• Spread the tomato paste over the pizza using the back of a spoon.

• Carefully cut the mozzarella ball into slices.

• Place the mozzarella slices onto the pizza (slightly overlapping) and scatter the tomatoes on the cheese.

• Bake the pizza in an oven preheated to 350°F (180°C) for 20 minutes.

• Garnish with a handful of torn, fresh basil leaves.

2

Hawaiian bites

These are a fun take on a ham and pineapple pizza. They'll be snapped up quickly, so make sure you try one before they're gone!

Ingredients

• pizza dough ball (from the recipe on pages 40–41)

• 2–3 tbsp tomato paste

• 8oz (227g) can pineapple chunks, drained

• 2oz (60g), cut into strips

• 1½ cups grated mozzarella

Method

• On a floured surface, divide your pizza dough into 12 small balls. Flatten the balls so they form small circles that are about 3in (8cm) in diameter.

• Spread the tomato paste over the dough circles using the back of a spoon.

• Place a couple of pineapple pieces and a few strips of ham onto each pizza.

• Sprinkle a little bit of grated mozzarella cheese over each pizza bite.

• Bake the pizzas in an oven preheated to 350°F (180°C) for 15 minutes.

Top this...

Check what you have in the pantry or fridge and try making up your own toppings for your pizza. Here are ideas for what you can use.

anchovies

baby spinach leaves

sliced bell peppers

pineapple

olives

chili peppers

pepperoni

cherry tomatoes

3

4

Mushroom madness

If you're a pizza fan, then this option will be right up your alley. The mushrooms and mozzarella will melt in your mouth.

Ingredients

- 1 tbsp olive oil
- 5oz (125g) mushrooms, sliced
- pizza dough ball (from the recipe on pages 40–41)
- 2–3 tbsp tomato paste
- large mozzarella ball

Method

- Gently heat the oil in a frying pan and fry the mushrooms for 2 minutes.
- Roll out your pizza dough on a floured surface into a circle that will fit your pizza pan. Roll the dough as thinly as you can.
- Spread the tomato paste over the pizza using the back of a spoon.
- Cut the mozzarella ball into thin slices.
- Place the mozzarella and mushrooms onto the pizza.
- Bake the pizzas in an oven preheated to 350°F (180°C) for 20 minutes.

Pizza pops

These fun lollipop-style pizzas are great for a party or picnic. The combination of bell peppers and tomatoes is delicious.

Ingredients

- pizza dough (from the recipe on 40–41)
- 2–3 tbsp tomato paste
- 1 cup grated mozzarella cheese
- half a yellow bell pepper, seeded and sliced
- 6 red plum or cherry tomatoes, halved
- 6 yellow cherry tomatoes, halved

Special equipment

- white ovenproof sticks

Method

- Divide your pizza dough into 12 small balls. Flatten the balls so they form small circles that are approximately 3 in (8 cm) in diameter. Insert a stick into each uncooked dough circle.
- Spread the tomato paste over the circles using the back of a spoon.
- Decorate with grated mozzarella, bell peppers, and tomatoes.
- Bake the pizzas in an oven preheated to 350°F (180°C) for 15 minutes.

Club sandwich

This triple-decker deluxe lunch uses ham, chicken, and cheese. But you can choose any ingredients you like to build your own stackable sandwich.

Serves 4   10 mins

Ingredients

- 6 slices white bread (you can use the bread from the Basic bread recipe, page 32)
- 4 tbsp mayonnaise
- 1 tbsp lemon juice
- 2oz (50g) iceberg lettuce, shredded
- 2 slices of ham
- 2 slices of Swiss or Cheddar cheese
- 1 tomato, sliced
- 2oz (50g) of cooked chicken breast, shredded

Equipment

- bread knife
- cutting board
- mixing bowl
- metal spoon
- toothpicks

1

Lightly toast the bread on both sides in a toaster or under a preheated broiler—ask an adult for help. Cut off the crusts.

2

In a small bowl, mix together the mayonnaise and lemon juice. Season to taste and then stir in the shredded lettuce.

3

Spread 2 slices of the white toast with half of the lettuce and mayonnaise mixture.

4

Place a slice of ham, then a slice of cheese on top of each. Top with another slice of toast and spread with the remaining lettuce and mayo.

5

Add some slices of tomato and the chicken. Top with the remaining toast.

6

Cut each sandwich into 4 triangles and secure each triangle with a toothpick.

Pita pockets

Tofu is a versatile and nutritious ingredient. The sauce used in this recipe gives the tofu a yummy barbecue taste, as well as an appealing glow.

In a shallow dish, mix together the ingredients for the marinade. Pat the tofu dry with paper towels and cut it into 8 long slices.

Put the tofu into the dish with the marinade. Spoon the marinade over the tofu until it is well coated. Marinate for at least 1 hour.

Brush the grill pan with a generous amount of olive oil and put it over high heat. Carefully place 4 of the tofu slices into the hot pan.

Cook the tofu for 4 minutes on each side, or until golden. As you cook, spoon more of the marinade over the top. Grill the rest of the tofu in the same way.

Ingredients
- 9oz (250g) firm tofu
- splash of olive oil
- 3 cos or romaine lettuce leaves, shredded
- 2 scallions, peeled and cut into long strips
- handful of alfalfa sprouts, optional
- 4 whole wheat pita breads, warmed in a toaster or oven

For the marinade
- 2 tbsp sweet chile sauce
- 2 tbsp ketchup
- 2 tbsp soy sauce
- ½ tsp ground cumin

Equipment
- small sharp knife
- cutting board
- paper towels
- tablespoon
- shallow dish
- grill pan
- spatula or tongs

5

Serves 4 80 mins 16 mins

Carefully slice along the edge of the pita bread. Divide the lettuce, scallions, and alfalfa sprouts between the pita bread and then add 2 pieces of tofu.

Variation

Strips of chicken, pork, turkey, or beef—or even a medley of vegetables such as pepper, zucchini, and onion—make a great alternative to the tofu.

Ingredients

- 1 cucumber
- 2 celery stalks
- 1 red bell pepper, seeded
- 1 yellow bell pepper, seeded
- 2 carrots
- 4 romaine or cos lettuce leaves
- 8 cherry tomatoes
- 4 broccoli florets

Sour cream and chive dip

- ½ cup sour cream
- 3 tbsp fresh chives, chopped
- 2 tsp lemon juice

Yogurt and mint dip

- 1 cup natural yogurt
- ½ cucumber, grated
- 2 tsp dried mint
- salt and freshly ground black pepper,

Equipment

- sharp knife
- cutting board
- 8 colorful cups and a platter, for serving vegetables
- 2 small glass bowls
- 2 tablespoons

Vegetable platter

This healthy, colorful snack works well for any occasion, and it's a perfect side to accompany a light meal.

Carefully slice the cucumber, celery stalks, peppers, and carrots into thin strips.

Place the vegetable sticks, lettuce leaves, broccoli florets, and cherry tomatoes into colorful cups on a platter and set aside.

Mix the sour cream, chives, and lemon juice in a small glass bowl. Pour into a colorful cup to serve.

In another small glass bowl, mix the natural yogurt, grated cucumber, and dried mint together. Season with salt and pepper. Serve in a colorful cup.

Alternatives

There are plenty of other vegetables and dips you can try out for a vegetable platter. Always wash vegetables thoroughly before preparing them.

Four ways with appetizers

Try out these these tasty bruschettas.

1

2

Tiny tomatoes

This is a delicious combination of ingredients and flavors. The mozzarella melts in your mouth and the tomatoes are so juicy.

Ingredients

This recipe is for 4 people. It takes 5 minutes to prepare and 2 minutes to cook.

· ciabatta loaf, sliced

· 5oz (125g) mini mozzarella balls

· 1 container plum or cherry tomatoes

· 8 fresh basil leaves

Method

● Toast the slices of ciabatta until golden. You may end up with 1 or 2 slices left over.

● Carefully slice the tomatoes in half.

● Place the mozzarella balls and tomatoes on the toasted slices of ciabatta.

● Scatter a few basil leaves on each slice of ciabatta.

● Serve as individual portions or on a large tray.

Crisscross ham

The salty ham and melted cheese make this bruschetta a yummy appetizer. It will be a real winner with your friends or family.

Ingredients

This recipe is for 4 people. It takes 5 minutes to prepare and 4 minutes to cook.

· ciabatta loaf, sliced

· 4¹/₂oz (125g) slices of ham

· 6oz (170g) Cheddar cheese

Method

● Toast the slices of ciabatta until golden. You may end up with 1 or 2 slices left over.

● Cut the ham into thin strips and the cheese into generous slices.

● Place the cheese slices onto the ciabatta and then add the ham in a crisscrossed pattern.

● Grill the bruschettas for 2 minutes, or until the cheese begins to bubble. Be careful not to let the ham overcook.

● Serve as individual portions or on a large tray.

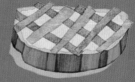

cheese

baby spinach leaves

red pepper

basil

roasted vegtables

salami

tomatoes

3

Carrot butter

The moist carrots and rich butter make this bruschetta a real favorite. You can keep any leftover mixture in the fridge for a few days.

Ingredients

This recipe is for 4 people. It takes 1 hour to prepare and 2 minutes to cook.

· ciabatta loaf, sliced

· 1 onion, finely chopped

· 4 carrots, finely grated

· 1 tsp tomato paste

· 1 tsp dried oregano

· 16 tbsp butter

· cilantro, to garnish

Method

• Over medium heat, fry the onions in a teaspoon of oil.

• Blend the onion, carrots, tomato paste, oregano, and butter in a food processor.

• Place the mixture in a bowl, cover, and refrigerate for 1 hour.

• Toast the slices of ciabatta until golden. You may have 1 or 2 slices left over.

• Generously spread the carrot butter onto the slices of toasted ciabatta and serve as individual portions or on a large platter.

• Garnish with cilantro, if desired.

4

Cheese and cucumber

These bright and fun bruschettas are great for parties. Use the remaining cucumber to make sticks to accompany the dish.

Ingredients

This recipe is for 4 people. It takes 5 minutes to prepare and 4 minutes to cook.

· ciabatta loaf, sliced

· 8oz (225g) cream cheese

· 1 cucumber

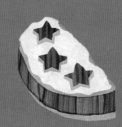

Method

• Toast the slices of ciabatta until golden. You may end up with 1 or 2 slices left over.

• Spread the cream cheese evenly over the bruschettas.

• Using a knife, carefully peel a cucumber. Use cookie cutters to make decorative shapes out of the peel and flesh of the cucumber.

• Place the shapes on the bruschettas and serve on individual plates or on a large platter.

51

MAIN MEALS

Serve in small casserole dishes

Lamb hotpot

Serves 6   25 mins   20 mins

This hotpot is a hearty main meal that will fill you up. The lamb and tomatoes make it juicy, and the chickpeas add texture. Serve it with crusty bread rolls.

Ingredients

- 6oz (175g) lean lamb (leg or fillet), cut into ¾in (2cm) cubes
- ½ tbsp all-purpose flour
- ¼ tsp paprika
- 1½ tbsp olive oil
- ½ large red onion, finely sliced
- 1½ garlic cloves, finely chopped
- ½ 14oz (400g) can chickpeas, drained and rinsed
- 14oz (400g) can chopped tomatoes
- freshly ground black pepper
- 5oz (125g) baby leaf spinach
- crusty bread rolls, to serve, optional

Equipment

- large glass bowl
- large pan
- wooden spoon
- 6 bowls or individual casserole dishes, for serving

Put the lamb, flour, and paprika into a mixing bowl and combine well so that the lamb is coated.

Heat the oil in a large pan over medium heat, add the onions, and cook, stirring often, for five minutes. Add the lamb and cook until browned.

Stir in the garlic and chickpeas, and cook for 1 minute. Add the tomatoes, bring to a boil, then simmer for 15 minutes.

Season well with freshly ground black pepper, stir in the spinach, and cook for 3 minutes.

Ingredients

- 2 apples
- 2 tbsp olive oil
- 6–8 sausages (turkey, pork, beef, or vegetarian)
- 1 onion, finely chopped
- 1 carrot, diced
- 2 cloves garlic, finely chopped
- 4oz (110g) lean bacon, cut into bite-sized pieces (optional)
- 1 tsp mixed herbs
- 14oz (400g) can borlotti or pinto beans, drained and rinsed
- ¼ cup canned chopped tomatoes
- 1 tbsp tomato paste
- salt and pepper
- 2 cups chicken or vegetable stock

Equipment

- vegetable peeler
- small sharp knife
- cutting board
- large ovenproof dish with lid (or large saucepan and large casserole dish with lid)
- oven mitts
- wooden spoon
- liquid measuring cup
- tongs

1 **Carefully remove** the peel from the apples using a vegetable peeler. Quarter the apples and remove the core. Cut them into bite-sized pieces and set aside.

2 **Preheat the oven** to 400°F (200°C). Heat the oil in a large saucepan or ovenproof dish and cook the sausages for 5 minutes, or until browned all over.

3 **Remove the sausages** from the pan and set aside. Put the onion and carrot into the pan and fry over medium heat for 5 minutes, stirring frequently.

4 **Next, add the garlic,** bacon, and herbs, stir well, and cook for 6 minutes. (Transfer to a large casserole dish if you aren't using an ovenproof dish.)

5 **Add the beans,** tomatoes, tomato paste, apples, and sausages and stir. Pour in the stock and bring to a boil.

6 **Cover with a lid** and place in the preheated oven. Cook for 25 minutes. The sauce will reduce and thicken and the apples will become tender.

Sausage hotpot

Fruit gives this savory dish a natural sweetness and an extra vitamin boost. Serve this winter warmer with fluffy mashed potatoes and steamed green vegetables.

Serves 4   20 mins   45 mins

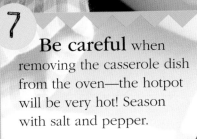

7

Be careful when removing the casserole dish from the oven—the hotpot will be very hot! Season with salt and pepper.

Serves 4   5 mins   10 mins

Beef pasta

This pasta dish is an easy main meal to make for you and your family. The combination of beef and mushrooms is super tasty.

Ingredients

- 1 small onion, finely chopped
- $1/2$ tbsp olive oil
- freshly ground black pepper
- 9oz (250g) lean ground beef
- 4oz (100g) mushrooms, chopped
- pinch of dried oregano
- 1 garlic clove, finely chopped
- 14oz (400g) can chopped tomatoes
- 1 tbsp tomato paste
- 1 tsp green pesto
- 7oz (200g) tortiglioni

Equipment

- frying pan
- wooden spoon
- saucepan
- colander

1

Cook the onion in the oil over low heat. Season with pepper, then stir in the ground beef and cook, stirring, until no longer pink.

2

Add the mushrooms, oregano, garlic, tomatoes, and tomato paste and stir well. Simmer for 10 minutes, then mix in the pesto.

3

Meanwhile, ask an adult to cook the pasta in a pan of boiling water. Using a colander, drain the pasta (over a bowl or sink), toss with the meat sauce, and serve.

Fresh tomato pasta

You don't need to cook the sauce for this pasta dish. It's deliciously fresh and fast to make. The classic flavors of tomato and basil are perfect together.

Ingredients

- 5 tomatoes, seeded and coarsely chopped
- 2 garlic cloves, finely chopped
- handful of basil leaves, torn
- 2 tbsp extra virgin olive oil
- freshly ground black pepper
- 7oz (200g) bow-tie pasta
- Parmesan cheese, freshly grated, to serve

Equipment

- large glass bowl
- wooden spoon
- large saucepan
- colander

Put the tomatoes, garlic, basil, and olive oil in a large bowl and season with pepper. Stir the mixture together using a wooden spoon.

Ask an adult to cook the pasta in a saucepan of boiling water according to the package instructions. Drain the pasta well in a colander. Toss with the tomato sauce and serve.

Serves 4   5 mins   10 mins

Ingredients

- 2 large red onions
- 2 large carrots, peeled
- 2 large zucchini
- 2 red bell peppers, seeded
- 1 medium eggplant
- 2 tsp chopped fresh rosemary
- 1 tbsp tomato paste
- 2 yellow bell peppers, seeded
- 14oz (400g) can chopped tomatoes
- salt and pepper
- 2 garlic cloves, crushed
- 1/4 cup olive oil
- 9 dried lasagne sheets

For the sauce:

- 2 cups warm milk
- 4 tbsp unsalted butter
- 1/4 cup all-purpose flour
- salt and pepper
- 1¼ cups grated Parmesan cheese

Equipment

- cutting board
- sharp knife
- roasting pan
- oven mitts
- large saucepan
- wooden spoon
- small saucepan
- whisk
- 10in x 7in x 2in (25cm x 18cm x 5cm) lasagne dish
- serving spoon

Vegetable lasagne

A crowd-pleasing dish that's a meal in its own right, this lasagne makes a welcome change from the meat-based version. Why not experiment with other flavors?

Ask an adult to preheat the oven to 425°F (220°C). Cut the onions into wedges and chop the other vegetables into chunks.

In the roasting pan, mix the oil, rosemary, and garlic with the vegetables and season. Roast for 35 minutes, shaking the pan occasionally.

Gently heat the tomatoes and tomato paste in a large saucepan. Take the pan off the heat and carefully stir in the roasted vegetables.

Over low heat, melt the butter in a small pan. Stir in the flour for 1 minute and whisk in the milk. Stir until thickened. Add half the cheese and season.

5

Serves 6 50 mins 1 hr 15 mins

Turn the oven down to 375°F (190°C). Spoon a third of the vegetables into the the dish and top with 3 lasagne sheets.

6

Add another third of the vegetables, top with another layer of lasagne, pour half the sauce over the top. Add the remaining vegetables.

7

Finally, lay the remaining lasagne sheets on top and drizzle the sauce over them. Sprinkle the cheese on top. Bake for 35 minutes, or until golden brown and bubbling.

Variations

Bring variety to this light
meal by adding a mixture
of steamed vegetables or a
fresh tossed salad of lettuce,
cherry tomatoes, and
cucumber slices.

Rice balls

Serves 4 • 30 mins • 5 mins

This dish works well as a light main meal or as a filling appetizer. The soft rice and melted mozzarella are tasty and have a great texture.

Ingredients

- 1¼ cups cold cooked Arborio or other risotto rice
- freshly ground black pepper
- 1 large ball buffalo mozzarella, cubed
- 1 egg, beaten
- 2 slices toast, for bread crumbs
- olive oil, for deep frying
- salsa, to serve
- salad, to serve

Equipment

- large glass bowl
- dinner plate
- spoon
- small bowl
- large dish
- large saucepan
- strainer
- paper towels

1 Generously season the rice with pepper and stir with a spoon to make sure the pepper is well dispersed. Roll the rice into 12 even-sized balls.

2 Push a cube of mozzarella cheese into the center of each ball, then cover so that the cheese is enclosed. Ask an adult to help if you find this step difficult.

Completely coat the balls

3 Roll each ball in the egg and then roll in the bread crumbs (bread or toast that's been turned into crumbs in a food processor—see page 9 for how to make bread crumbs).

4 Ask an adult to deep-fry the balls in olive oil over medium heat for 2–3 minutes, or until golden brown. Be extra careful around hot oil.

61

Jambalaya

This is a colorful Creole or Cajun rice dish from Louisiana. It is easy to make because all the ingredients are cooked in the same pot.

Serves 4   20 mins   50 mins

Ingredients

- 2 tbsp olive oil
- 3 skinless, boneless chicken breasts
- 1 large onion, finely chopped
- 7oz (200g) smoked ham
- 2 large cloves garlic, chopped
- 1 red bell pepper, seeded and cut into bite-sized pieces
- 1 tsp paprika
- 1 jalapeño pepper, seeded and finely chopped (optional)
- 1 tsp dried thyme
- 2½ cups warm chicken or vegetable stock
- 3 tbsp canned chopped tomatoes
- 1½ cups brown rice
- ½ cup peas
- salt and pepper

Equipment

- strainer
- small sharp knife
- cutting board
- large saucepan with lid
- wooden spoon

1

Put the rice in a strainer and rinse it under cold water until the water runs clear. Washing the rice before cooking keeps it from becoming sticky.

2

Chop the onion into small pieces and set aside. Carefully cut the chicken and ham into bite-sized pieces. Heat the oil in the large saucepan.

3

Fry the chicken and onion for 8 minutes over medium heat, until the chicken is golden brown all over. Stir frequently so it doesn't stick to the pan.

4

Add the ham, garlic, red bell pepper, and jalapeño (if using). Cook for 2 minutes. Add the paprika, thyme, rice, stock, and tomatoes. Stir. Bring to a boil.

5

Reduce the heat to low and cover the pan. Simmer for 35 minutes, or until the rice is cooked and the water is absorbed. Season to taste and stir before serving.

Variations

The recipe can easily be adapted for vegetarians by replacing the chicken and ham with extra vegetables, meat-free sausages, beans, or tofu.

Potato salad

This simple potato salad is a classic. It replaces the traditional mayonnaise with a light, creamy sauce flavored with fresh chives.

Ingredients

- 1¼lb (500g) baby new potatoes
- 3 tbsp low-fat crème fraîche
- 3 tbsp low-fat yogurt
- 2 tbsp freshly chopped chives

Equipment

- knife
- cutting board
- saucepan
- 2 mixing bowls
- metal spoon

Wash the potatoes thoroughly. Make sure there's no dirt left on them. Cut any larger potatoes in half.

Cook in a pan of lightly salted boiling water for 12–15 minutes. Drain and allow to cool. Place in a mixing bowl.

In a small bowl, mix together the crème fraîche, yogurt, and fresh chives.

Gently stir the chive mixture into the potatoes. Season to taste. Keep refrigerated until ready to serve.

Fishcakes

Serves 4   15 mins   25 mins

Potatoes can be cooked in many ways: mashed, boiled, roasted, and baked. Bite into these crunchy fishcakes and the creamy fish and mashed potatoes will melt in your mouth.

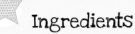

Ingredients

- 10oz (250g) smoked haddock
- 1 fresh bay leaf
- 1½ cups milk
- ¾lb (375g) potatoes, unpeeled, boiled, and mashed
- 8 scallions, finely chopped
- ⅔ cup corn kernels
- 4 eggs, hard-boiled
- 2 tbsp fresh parsley, chopped
- zest of 1 lemon
- ½ cup heavy cream
- 2 egg yolks
- 2 eggs
- ¾ cup flour

- 1 cup fresh bread crumbs
- 1 tbsp butter
- 2 tbsp olive oil
- salsa, to serve
- lemon wedges, to serve

Equipment

- shallow pan
- large mixing bowl
- fork
- spoon
- 2 small glass bowls
- whisk
- cutting board
- large shallow bowl
- large plate
- frying pan
- spatula

1

Cook the haddock fillets with the bay leaf and the milk in a shallow pan. Let them simmer for 5–10 minutes. Cool, then remove the fish skin and any bones, and flake the haddock into chunks.

2

Combine the fish, potatoes, scallions, corn, eggs, parsley, and lemon zest. In a small bowl, beat the heavy cream with the egg yolks, and stir into the mixture.

3

Divide the mixture into four parts. Shape each part into a slightly flattened ball. Roll each fishcake in the flour on a plate. Shake off any excess.

4

Crack two eggs into a small bowl and whisk. Transfer to a large shallow bowl. Dip each fishcake into the eggs so that they are thoroughly coated.

5

Coat the fishcakes well in the fresh bread crumbs. Make sure the fishcakes are completely covered in bread crumbs.

6

Heat the oil and butter in a frying pan and carefully add the fishcakes. Fry them gently for about 4–5 minutes on each side, or until golden brown.

Mashed potato pies

This dish is filling and nutritious. You can make it with ground beef, pork, or lamb, or make a vegetarian version. If you don't have four small dishes, use one large dish instead.

1

Preheat the oven to 400°F (200°C). Peel and dice the onion and carrot. Crush the garlic.

2

Heat the oil and fry the beef for 4 minutes, or until browned, stirring constantly. Add the onion, carrot, rosemary, and garlic and fry for 3–5 minutes.

3

Add the mushrooms, stock, tomato paste, Worcestershire sauce, and tomatoes. Bring to a boil. Reduce heat; simmer for 20 minutes. Season with salt and pepper.

4

Half-fill a pan with water and bring it to a boil. Peel and chop the potatoes and add them to the pan, along with the salt. Boil for 12–15 minutes, or until soft.

5

Drain the potatoes in a colander and put them back into the saucepan. Mash the potatoes with the milk, butter, and half the cheese.

6

Place the dishes on a baking sheet and divide the meat filling equally among them. Top each with mashed potato and the remaining cheese. Bake for 25–30 minutes, or until golden.

Ingredients

- 1 onion
- 1 carrot
- 1 garlic clove
- 1 tbsp olive oil
- 1lb 2oz (500g) lean ground beef
- 2 tsp rosemary, chopped, optional
- 5oz (125g) mushrooms, quartered
- ⅔ cup beef stock
- 1 tbsp tomato paste
- 2 tsp Worcestershire sauce, optional
- 14oz (400g) can chopped tomatoes

Topping

- 1¼lb (550g) potatoes
- pinch of salt
- 2 tbsp milk
- 1 tbsp unsalted butter
- 3oz (75g) cheese, grated

Equipment

- oven mitts
- cutting board
- vegetable peeler
- sharp knife
- garlic crusher
- 2 large saucepans
- wooden spoon
- colander
- potato masher
- four ovenproof dishes
- large baking sheet
- fork
- tablespoon

Serves 6   30 mins   40 mins

You can serve this dish with salsa and tortilla chips.

Chili con carne

This meal has a real kick to it, so if you don't like your food too spicy then you should use less of the jalapeño pepper. The meat and beans are full of protein and very filling. You can keep any leftovers in the refrigerator for the next day.

Ingredients
- 1½ large onions, diced
- 9oz (250g) lean ground beef
- 1 garlic clove, finely chopped
- ½ jalapeño pepper, finely chopped
- ¼ tsp chili powder
- ¼ tsp paprika
- 15oz (425g) can red kidney beans, drained and rinsed
- 1 bay leaf
- 14.5oz (400g) can chopped tomatoes
- ½ tsp dried oregano
- ground black pepper
- basmati rice, to serve

Equipment
- frying pan
- wooden spoon
- colander
- glass bowl
- four small bowls or dishes for serving

Cook the onions and meat for 5 minutes. Stir in the garlic, jalapeño, chili powder, and paprika, and cook for 5 more minutes.

Add the kidney beans and bay leaf, and fry for 2 minutes. Always be extra careful when near a hot stove. Ask an adult to help you.

Add the tomatoes and oregano. Bring to a boil, season with pepper, then simmer on low heat for 40 minutes, stirring occasionally.

Ask an adult to cook the rice according to the method on the package. Drain using a colander. Take the bay leaf out of the chili.

Ingredients

- 9oz (250g) lean ground beef
- 2oz (50g) Parmesan cheese, freshly grated
- 1 cup fresh bread crumbs, cubed
- 1½ tbsp olive oil
- ½ garlic clove, crushed
- ½ onion, finely chopped
- 1 egg
- 1 tsp dried oregano
- olive oil, for frying
- 16 miniature bread rolls
- 2 tomatoes, thinly sliced
- lettuce leaves
- 14oz (400g) jar tomato sauce or salsa

Equipment

- large glass bowl
- baking sheet
- wax paper
- frying pan
- spatula
- cutting board
- knife
- skewers (to hold hamburgers together)

Mini burgers

These mini-burgers are hard to beat. Once you make them for your family and friends, they'll soon be asking when you're going to serve them again!

Prepare a baking sheet with a piece of wax paper. Use your hands to mix all the ingredients for the hamburgers: beef, Parmesan, bread crumbs, oil, garlic, onion, egg, and oregano.

Form the mixture into balls about the size of walnuts and flatten them slightly. Chill them in the fridge for 30 minutes. Wash your hands well after handling raw meat.

Fry the hamburgers in oil over medium heat. Turn over after 5 minutes. Put a fork in the meat; if the juice is clear, then they're done.

Carefully cut the rolls in half. Fill each roll with a cooked hamburger, a tomato slice, a lettuce leaf, and tomato sauce.

Serves 6   30 mins   15 mins

BBQ chicken

On a summer's day you can cook this meal on the barbecue. The chicken also tastes good when cooked under the broiler. It's the marinade that provides the flavor.

Ingredients

- 2 tbsp ketchup
- 2 tbsp soy sauce
- 2 tbsp fresh orange juice
- 1 tbsp sunflower oil
- 3 tbsp honey
- 1 garlic clove, crushed
- 1 tsp mustard
- 8 chicken drumsticks

Equipment

- small mixing bowl
- whisk
- paper towels
- sharp knife
- cutting board
- plastic wrap
- oven mitts
- foil-lined broiling pan
- tongs
- tablespoon
- large dish, about 2in (5cm) deep

Place all the ingredients, except the chicken drumsticks, into a bowl and whisk them together. Pour the mixture into a large, shallow dish.

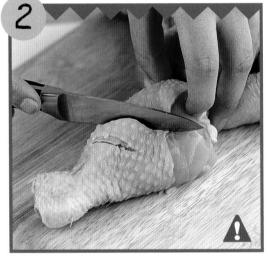

Pat the chicken pieces with paper towels. Make 3 deep cuts in each drumstick. This is known as scoring and helps the meat to soak up the marinade.

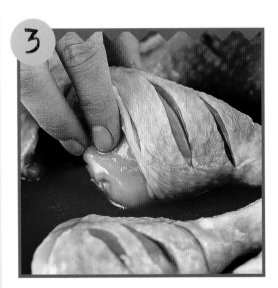

Place the chicken in the marinade and roll each piece until it is coated. Cover the dish with plastic wrap and let it marinate in the fridge for 1 hour.

Preheat the oven to 350°F (180°C). Lay the coated chicken (uncut-side up) on a foil-lined broiling pan. Put the marinade to one side. Bake the chicken for 20–25 minutes and baste it with leftover marinade halfway through.

Serves 4   75 mins   28-35 mins

5

Turn the oven off
and preheat the broiler.
Baste the chicken pieces and
finish cooking them under
the broiler for 8–10 minutes.

6

Using tongs, turn the
chicken over halfway through
broiling and baste it with
marinade. This helps to
keep it moist.

Cook until crispy on top

Four ways with Kebabs

Kebabs are fun and really easy to make.

Chicken satay

This is a popular kebab recipe. Always soak the wooden skewers in cold water for 30 minutes to prevent them from burning.

Ingredients

This recipe is for 4 people. It takes 20 minutes to prepare and 16 minutes to cook.

• 1lb 2oz (500g) skinless, boneless chicken breasts

• $^{1}/_{2}$ lime, cut into wedges, to serve

• Follow the recipe on page 82 for the satay sauce

> To make sure the chicken is fully cooked, pierce it with a fork to see if the juices run clear.

Method

• Make the satay sauce in a large bowl and set aside. Save a small amount to use as a dip.

• Cut up the chicken breasts into large chunks 1$^{1}/_{2}$in (4cm) cubes and place into the large bowl of satay sauce. Marinate in the fridge for 1 hour.

• Thread the chicken chunks onto short skewers (or large skewers cut in half). Discard any remaining marinade.

• Place the kebabs on a broiler pan and cook for about 8 minutes. Turn over and cook for another 8 minutes. Serve the chicken warm with the satay sauce for dipping and wedges of lime.

Ingredients

This recipe is for 4 people. It takes 80 minutes to prepare and 20 minutes to cook.

For the kebabs

• 9oz (250g) firm tofu

• 2 small zucchini, each cut into 8 wedges

• 2 medium red onions, each cut into 8 wedges

• 1 medium red bell pepper, seeded and cut into 16 chunks

For the marinade

• 2 tbsp olive oil

• 1 tbsp soy sauce

• 3 tbsp black bean sauce

• 1 tbsp honey

• 2 garlic cloves, crushed

• salad, to serve

Tofu chunks

This colorful kebab makes a perfect vegetarian option for a summer barbecue.

Method

• Cut the tofu into 16 cubes. Put the cubes into a dish with the zucchini, onions, and red bell pepper.

• Mix the ingredients for the marinade in a large dish. Season with salt and pepper. Use a spoon to coat the tofu and vegetables in marinade. Put in the fridge for 1 hour.

• Thread the vegetables and tofu onto 8 skewers.

• Place the kebabs on the barbecue and brush them with the marinade. Grill for 15–20 minutes, turning them halfway through and brushing them with more marinade.

yellow zucchini

mushrooms

onions

halloumi cheese

eggplant

Try your own

Play around with combinations of ingredients to make up your own kebabs. Use the barbecue sauce from page 82 to create a beef and onion combo. You can use the items pictured here, although not all on one skewer!

3

4

Lamb with mint yogurt

Lamb is delicious when flavored with herbs and spices. You can make a mint and yogurt dip to accompany this classic kebab.

Ingredients

This recipe is for 4 people. It takes 20 minutes to prepare and 20 minutes to cook.

· 1lb (450g) ground lamb

· 1 small onion, finely chopped

· 1 garlic clove

· ¹/₂ tsp ground cinnamon

· 2 tsp ground cumin

· 1 tsp ground coriander

· olive oil, for brushing

· 1 tsp dried mint

· ¹/₂ lemon, to serve

· Follow the recipe on page 48 for the yogurt and mint dip

Method

● Put the ground lamb in a mixing bowl. Add the chopped onion, garlic, cinnamon, cumin, and coriander to the bowl. Stir the ingredients until they are all combined.

● Divide the lamb mixture into 12 pieces. Shape each one into a sausage and then thread the sausages onto the skewers. Press or roll to lengthen the kebabs.

● Place the lamb kebabs onto the baking sheet and brush them with oil. Broil for about 2 minutes on each side, until golden. Transfer to a serving dish and sprinkle with mint. Serve with a yoghurt and mint dip and lemon wedges.

Shrimp and bell peppers

This bright and colorful kebab is full of flavor. Squeeze lime juice over the top to serve.

Ingredients

This recipe is for 4 people. It takes 25 minutes to prepare and 15 minutes to cook.

For the marinade

· juice of 1 lemon

· juice of 1 lime

· 2 tbsp soy sauce

· 1 garlic clove, crushed

· 1 tsp light brown sugar

For the kebabs

· ¹/₂ red bell pepper

· ¹/₂ yellow bell pepper

· 8 cherry tomatoes

· 4 baby corncobs

· 5¹/₂ oz (150g) cooked shrimp

Method

● Make the marinade by mixing the ingredients together in a liquid measuring cup. Carefully cut the peppers and baby corncob into chunks.

● Thread the vegetables and shrimp onto the skewers. Place the kebabs into a rectangular dish. Pour the marinade over the top. Put the kebabs into the refrigerator for an hour. Turn them over after 30 minutes.

● Broil the kebabs for 15 minutes. Baste the shrimp every five minutes with the marinade (discard any leftover marinade).

Vegetable tart

This dish is best served cold. It's perfect for a light evening meal or for lunch. Serve it with potato salad and a green salad.

Serves 6   135 mins   65 mins

Equipment

- stainer
- mixing bowl
- knife
- fork
- tablespoon
- plastic wrap
- rolling pin
- 8in (20cm) fluted pie pan with removable bottom
- table knife
- wax paper
- baking beans or dried kidney beans
- oven mitt
- liquid measuring cup
- whisk

Ingredients

- 1³/₄ all-purpose flour, plus extra for dusting
- pinch of salt
- 6 tbsp unsalted butter, cubed
- 2 tbsp vegetable shortening or lard, diced
- 2 tbsp water
- ³/₄ red bell peppers, seeded and diced
- ³/₄ cup corn
- ³/₄ cup peas
- 1 small leek, sliced and sautéed
- 2 eggs, beaten
- ¹/₂ cup milk
- ¹/₂ cup light cream
- ¹/₄ cup grated Cheddar cheese

1

Sift the flour and salt into a bowl. Stir in the butter and shortening (or lard), until coated. Rub into the flour.

2

Once the mixture looks like crumbs, add the water, drop by drop, and stir with a knife. When the crumbs start to come together, gather the dough in your hands.

3

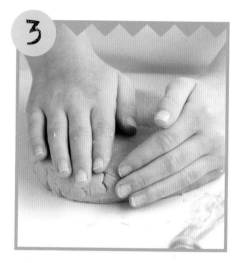

Shape the dough into a smooth disk and wrap it in plastic wrap. Chill for 1 hour in the fridge, or until firm. Next lightly flour your work surface.

4

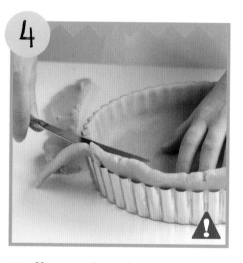

Roll out the dough so that it is slightly bigger than the pan. Gently press it into the pan and use a knife to trim off the excess. Use a fork to prick the crust and chill it again for 15 minutes. Preheat the oven to 400°F (200°C).

5

Cover the tart with 2 layers of wax paper and add the baking beans. Bake for 15 minutes, remove the paper and beans and bake for another 5 minutes. This technique is called baking blind and it helps the crust stay firm when the wet filling is added.

6

Ask an adult to turn the oven down to 350°F (180°C). Scatter the vegetables over the crust. Whisk the eggs, milk, and cream together and pour into the tart. Sprinkle the cheese over the top and bake for 45 minutes. Allow the tart to set and cool before serving.

Tomato and eggplant layers

Slow roasted tomatoes are chewy, juicy, and tasty. Everyone who tries this dish will love the combination of textures and flavors.

Ingredients

- 6 large ripe tomatoes, cut in half
- 2 garlic cloves, finely chopped
- 1 tbsp dried oregano
- 1/2 cup extra virgin olive oil
- 1 large eggplant, thinly sliced
- pinch of smoked paprika
- 1/2 cup natural yogurt
- 2 tbsp honey
- 1/4 cup sliced almonds

Equipment

- baking sheet
- spoon
- colander
- large bowl
- grill pan
- 4 serving dishes

Lay the tomatoes cut-side up on the sheet. In a small bowl, mix the garlic and oregano, half of the olive oil, and season with salt and pepper. Spoon it over the tomatoes.

Preheat the oven to 300°F (150°C). Bake the tomatoes for 2–3 hours. When ready, they should be slightly shriveled, but still a brilliant red color. Let cool.

Layer the slices of eggplant in a colander, sprinkling a little salt between each layer. Leave for 30 minutes, then rinse well with water and pat dry with paper towels.

Place the eggplant slices in a large bowl, pour the rest of the olive oil over the top, and sprinkle with paprika. Toss together with your hands.

Serves 4 40 mins 190 mins

5

Heat a ridged grill pan, then add a single layer of the eggplant slices. Cook each side until tender. Place the slices on a plate. Repeat for the other slices.

6

To serve, layer the tomatoes and eggplant in 4 dishes. Drizzle two tablespoons of yogurt and half a tbsp of honey over each dish. Sprinkle half a tablespoon of almonds over each portion.

Four ways with sauces

Try these simple and versatile sauces.

1

Chunky tomato sauce

This sauce is hearty and full of flavor. It can be used in a lasagne if you double the quantities or as a simple sauce for a pasta dish.

Ingredients

This recipe is for 4 people. It takes 3 minutes to prepare and 5 minutes to cook.

• 1 onion

• 1 garlic clove

• 2 tbsp olive oil

• 14oz (400g) can chopped tomatoes

• 1 tbsp tomato paste

Method

• Chop the onion into small pieces and crush the garlic clove.

• Pour the oil into a saucepan and add the onion and garlic. Fry gently for 2 minutes, or until the onion is golden.

• Add the canned tomatoes and tomato paste to the saucepan. Stir and cook for 3 minutes.

2

Crunchy satay sauce

You can use smooth peanut butter for this classic sauce, but crunchy peanut butter gives it a better texture.

Ingredients

This recipe is for 4 people. It takes 5 minutes to prepare and 6 minutes to cook.

• 1½ onions

• 1½ in (3cm) fresh ginger

• 3 garlic clove

• ¼ cup vegetable oil

• 3 tbsp soy sauce

• 9 tbsp water

• ¼ cup light brown sugar

• 1 cup crunchy peanut butter

• juice of 2 limes

Method

• Peel the onions and chop them very finely.

• Peel the ginger and grate it coarsely. Peel and crush the garlic.

• Heat the oil in a saucepan. Cook the onion gently for 3 minutes, or until soft. Add the ginger and garlic and cook for a few minutes. Allow the mixture to cool.

• Put the onion mixture, soy sauce, water, sugar, peanut butter, and lime juice in a bowl and whisk.

• This recipe is perfect for chicken kebabs (see page 76).

Get these tools...

As the name suggests, a saucepan is used for making sauces. You will need these items to make most sauces. The wooden spoon is for stirring and the whisk is for blending the ingredients together.

saucepan

wooden spoon

whisk

knife

3

4

Cheesy white sauce

This sauce is often used in lasagne (see 58–59). You can also put it on pasta and add cooked bacon to make a cheesy, creamy pasta.

Ingredients

This recipe is for 6 people (when used in a lasagne). It takes 5 minutes to prepare and 6 minutes to cook.

- 4 tbsp unsalted butter
- ¼ cup all-purpose flour
- 2 cups warm milk
- ⅔ cup grated Parmesan cheese
- salt and pepper

Method

- Over low heat, melt the butter in a small pan.
- Stir in the flour and cook for 1 minute. Gradually whisk in the milk. Stir and continue heating until thickened.
- Add the cheese and season with salt and pepper. Stir until the cheese is well mixed into the sauce.

Barbecue sauce

Tasty and sweet, this sauce uses the natural sugars from oranges and honey to give it a delicious flavor.

Ingredients

This recipe is for 6 people. It takes 10 minutes to prepare and works perfectly for a marinade.

- 2 garlic cloves
- ¼ cup ketchup
- ¼ cup soy sauce
- ¼ cup fresh orange juice
- 2 tbsp sunflower oil
- 6 tbsp honey
- 2 tsp mustard

Method

- Crush the garlic cloves and put in a glass bowl.
- Add the ketchup, soy sauce, and orange juice to the bowl and mix well with a wooden spoon.
- Pour in the sunflower oil, honey, and mustard. Mix all the ingredients for 2 minutes or until everything has blended into a sauce.
- This recipe has double quantities of the BBQ chicken recipe on pages 74–75. Use it as a marinade to flavor meat or vegetables.

Mixed bean stir-fry

Serves 4 · 30 mins · 10 mins

This vegetarian stir-fry is incredibly tasty and quick to cook. The dessicated coconut and cashew nuts give it a crunchy texture and delicious flavor.

Ingredients

- ²/₃ cup unsweetened, dried coconut
- 2 tbsp sunflower oil
- 1 garlic clove, sliced
- 6 scallions, chopped
- 1 fennel bulb, sliced, core removed
- 1lb 2oz (500g) green and pole beans, thinly sliced
- 2 tbsp soy sauce
- 1 tbsp rice vinegar
- 4oz (100g) beansprouts
- 1 tbsp cilantro, finely chopped
- 7oz (200g) whole wheat noodles
- 1 tbsp sesame seeds
- 3oz (75g) unsalted cashew nuts

Place the coconut in a bowl of warm water, cover, and leave for 20 minutes. Strain the coconut through a strainer, pressing it against the sides.

Heat the oil in a large frying pan or wok. Add the garlic, onion, and fennel. Using a wooden spoon stir all the time for about 2 minutes.

Add your sliced beans and fry quickly, stirring all the time. Pour in the soy sauce and vinegar. Stir well, then remove the pan from the heat.

Add the beansprouts to the stir-fry. Sprinkle in the coconut and cilantro. Then stir the mixture thoroughly. Mmm! Smells good.

Cook the noodles following the instructions on the package. Drain the noodles well using a colander, then spoon them into your serving bowls.

Spoon the stir-fry onto the top of the noodles. After roasting the cashew nuts and sesame seeds, sprinkle on top and serve.

Rainbow beef

Stir-frying is a quick and easy way to make a colorful and nutritious meal. You can serve it on its own or eat it with rice or noodles.

Ingredients

- 10oz (300g) lean beef, cut into thin strips
- 1 tbsp sunflower oil
- 1 red bell pepper, seeded and cut into thin strips
- 6 baby corn, halved
- 3oz (75g) snow peas
- 3 scallions, sliced on the diagonal
- 2 cloves garlic, chopped
- 2 tsp grated fresh ginger
- ¼ cup fresh orange juice

Marinade

- 6 tbsp hoisin sauce
- 2 tbsp soy sauce
- 1 tbsp honey
- 1 tsp sesame oil

Equipment

- small sharp knife
- cutting board
- spoon
- shallow dish
- wok or large frying pan
- spatula or wooden spoon
- tongs

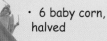

Put the marinade ingredients in a shallow dish. Mix them together and then add the beef strips. Coat the beef in the marinade, cover, and set aside for 1 hour.

Heat the sunflower oil in a wok or frying pan. Remove the beef from the marinade using tongs and carefully put it into a wok or frying pan.

Stirring continuously, fry the beef on high heat for 1–2 minutes, or until browned all over. Remove the beef using the tongs and set aside.

Pour a little more oil into the wok if it looks dry. Add the red bell pepper, baby corn, snow peas, and scallions. Stir-fry for 2 minutes.

5

Serves 4   80 mins   10 mins

Add the garlic, ginger, beef, and leftover marinade and stir-fry for 1 minute. Pour in the orange juice and cook, stirring regularly, for another minute.

Variations

Strips of pork and chicken are a good alternative to the beef. You can also use shrimp or tofu in the recipe. For the best flavor, remember to marinate first!

Marinated chicken

The chicken in this recipe is marinated so that it absorbs the curry flavor. If you want a stronger flavor you can marinate the meat for longer than 30 minutes.

1

In a bowl, mix the tomato paste, oil, and curry powder together to make a paste. Add the lemon juice and half the yogurt to make the marinade.

2

Carefully cut each chicken breast into cubes of about 1in (2.5cm). Always wash your hands after handling raw meat.

3

Stir the chicken into the marinade, season with salt and pepper, and cover the bowl. Let the chicken marinate in the refrigerator for 30 minutes.

4

Place the frying pan over medium to high heat and fry the chicken for 3–4 minutes. The chicken will change color but it will not be cooked.

5

Add the golden raisins and almonds and cook for 3–4 minutes. Before serving, cut a piece of chicken in half. If there is no trace of pink, it is cooked.

6

To shred the lettuce, roll up the leaves and carefully cut them into thin slices. Serve the chicken with the shredded lettuce, naan bread, and mango chutney.

Ingredients

- 1 tsp tomato paste
- 2 tbsp vegetable oil
- 1 tbsp curry powder
- juice of ½ lemon
- ½ cup natural yogurt

- 2 boneless, skinless chicken breasts
- salt and pepper
- ½ cup golden raisins, optional
- ½ cup slivered almonds, optional

To serve
- 1 head Little Gem or cos lettuce
- naan bread
- 2 tbsp mango chutney, optional

Equipment

- mixing bowl
- tablespoon
- 2 cutting boards
- 2 sharp knives
- frying pan
- wooden spatula

Serves 4   50 mins   10 mins

Four ways with roasted vegetables

Each of these dishes can accompany a main meal.

1

Reds and greens

This vegetable medley is colorful and has a slight crunch. It can be paired nicely with the Rice balls or Grilled chicken.

Ingredients

This recipe is for 4 people when served as a side dish. It takes 8 minutes to prepare and 50–60 minutes to cook.

1 red onion

2 whole raw beets, peeled

½ head broccoli

10 cherry tomatoes

1 tbsp olive oil

Method

• Preheat the oven to 400°F (200°C).

• On a cutting board, use a sharp knife to cut the red onion into large chunks. Slice the beets into large wedges, and cut the florets off the broccoli.

• Place the beets into a roasting pan or ovenproof dish and, using your hands, toss them in oil. Cook for 20 minutes.

• Add the remaining ingredients and cook for another 30–40 minutes.

2

Sweet potato and parsnip

This dish works well with the lamb or sausage hotpot. It will warm you on a cold day.

Ingredients

This recipe is for 4 people when served as a side dish. It takes 5 minutes to prepare and 50 minutes to cook.

2 large sweet potatoes, peeled

3 parsnips, peeled

1 tbsp olive oil

Method

• Preheat the oven to 400°F (200°C).

• On a cutting board, use a sharp knife to cut the parsnips into large chunks. Slice the sweet potatoes into wedges.

• Put the parsnips and potatoes into a roasting pan or an ovenproof dish and, using your hands, toss the vegetables in oil.

• Roast in the oven for 50 minutes, or until the vegetables are golden.

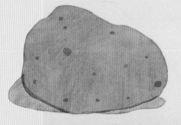

Try your own

There are plenty of other vegetables that taste delicious when roasted and work well as a side for any main dish. Try these other ingredients.

tomatoes · mushrooms · butternut squash · leeks · olives

3

4

Bell pepper medley

The roasted garlic is really tasty, while the bell peppers are juicy and full of flavor. This dish pairs nicely with the Marinated chicken.

Ingredients

This recipe is for 4 people when served as a side dish. It takes 8 minutes to prepare and 40 minutes to cook.

1 green bell pepper

1 yellow bell pepper

1 red bell pepper

1 orange bell pepper

1 garlic clove

1 small zucchini

1 tbsp olive oil

Method

- Preheat the oven to 400°F (200°C).

- On a cutting board, use a sharp knife to slice the peppers into thin strips and cut the garlic in half.

- Carefully cut the zucchini into thick slices.

- Place all the ingredients in a roasting pan or ovenproof dish and, using your hands, toss everything in oil.

- Cook for 40 minutes.

Roast potato and carrot

This is the classic combination of roasted vegetables that is often served with Roast chicken. It adds carbohydrates to a light meal.

Ingredients

This recipe is for 4 people when served as a side dish. It takes 5 minutes to prepare and 50 minutes to cook.

10 small (or 5 large) carrots

5 small potatoes, peeled

Method

- Preheat the oven to 400°F (200°C).

- On a cutting board, use a sharp knife to quarter the potatoes and cut the carrots into thick wedges.

- Place the potatoes and carrots in a roasting pan or ovenproof dish and, using your hands, toss them in oil.

- Cook for 50 minutes, or until the vegetables are golden.

Ingredients

- 3lb (1.5kg) whole chicken
- 5 tbsp unsalted butter, softened
- salt and pepper
- ½ lemon and 1 tsp lemon zest
- 1 tbsp fresh thyme leaves, plus 2 sprigs
- 1 large onion, chopped
- 8 mini carrots
- 1 garlic bulb
- 1 cup vegetable stock

To Serve

- 12 broccoli florets, boiled and drained
- 4 potatoes, chopped into quarters and roasted
- 16 mini carrots, roasted
- 1 cup gravy

Equipment

- plastic cutting board
- paper towels
- small mixing bowl
- 2 tablespoons
- sharp knife
- string
- roasting pan
- oven mitts
- large wooden cutting board
- carving knife

Roast chicken

Everyone loves a traditional roast chicken for dinner. This is a classic recipe that you can easily master and use for the rest of your life. You'll definitely impress your family when you make it.

Preheat the oven to 400°F (200°C). Rinse inside the chicken with cold water. Place it on a plastic cutting board and pat it dry, inside and out, with paper towels.

To make the stuffing, mix the softened butter with the thyme leaves, lemon zest, salt, and pepper in a bowl. Place inside the chicken, with the lemon and thyme sprigs.

Put the chicken into a roasting pan on a bed of onions, carrot, garlic, and vegetable stock. Roast it for 1 hour 20 minutes, or until golden brown. Baste the meat after 30 minutes and then every 15 minutes after that.

Carefully transfer the cooked chicken to a rack and let rest for 10–15 minutes before carving. Serve with, gravy, broccoli, roasted potatoes, and carrots.

Extras

Use the recipe on page 91 for roast potatoes and carrots. Boil the broccoli florets for 5 minutes; drain and serve. Make 1 cup gravy to serve with your meal.

Serves 4   30 mins   80 mins

Grilled chicken

Food has an wonderful texture and finish to it when it's been cooked in a grill pan. Always make sure you cook the meat thoroughly. You can eat this dish hot or cold.

Serves 4 45 mins 25 mins

Ingredients

- 2 tsp paprika
- 5 tbsp olive oil
- 4 skinless, boneless chicken breasts, each about 5½oz (150g)
- 14oz (400g) new potatoes, cut in half, if necessary
- 2 scallions, finely chopped

- 8 cherry tomatoes, halved
- 3 tbsp chopped fresh mint
- 1 tbsp lemon juice

Equipment

- large shallow dish
- tablespoon
- plastic wrap

- grill pan
- tongs
- small sharp knife
- cutting board
- medium saucepan
- colander
- large glass bowl

1

Mix the paprika and 3 tablespoons of olive oil in a large dish. Add the chicken and spoon the marinade over the top. Cover with plastic wrap. Chill for 30 minutes.

2

Heat a grill pan until it is very hot. Reduce the heat to medium and place 2 chicken breasts in the pan. Grill for 6 minutes on one side.

3

Carefully turn the chicken over using tongs. Spoon some of the marinade over the top and cook for 6 minutes, or until cooked through. Grill the remaining chicken.

4

Put the potatoes in a medium saucepan and cover with water. Bring to a boil and cook the potatoes for 10 minutes, or until they are tender.

5

Drain the potatoes and let them cool in a bowl. Add the mint to the bowl of potatoes.

6

Mix the olive oil and lemon juice together, using a fork. Then pour the dressing over the potato salad and stir to mix it well.

SWEET THINGS

Ingredients

- 8oz (225g) store-bought pie dough
- 6oz (150g) mascarpone cheese
- ½ tsp pure vanilla extract
- 2 tbsp confectioners' sugar
- 6oz (175g) strawberries
- ¼ cup red currant (or raspberry) jelly
- 1 tbsp water

Equipment

- rolling pin
- 3½in (9cm) fluted pastry cutter
- 12-hole muffin pan
- parchment paper
- dried beans or chickpeas
- oven mitts
- cooling rack
- small mixing bowl
- wooden spoon
- strainer
- cutting board
- sharp knife
- teaspoon
- small saucepan
- pastry brush

Strawberry tarts

These pretty pastries taste as good as they look! You can also make them with other types of soft fruit.

Makes 8   20 mins   13 mins

Preheat the oven to 400°F (200°C). Roll out the pastry until it is ¼in (7mm) thick. Using the fluted pastry cutter, cut out 8 circles. Press the pastry circles into a muffin pan.

Line the crusts with parchment paper and fill them with dried beans. Cook for 10 minutes, then remove the beans. Return to the oven for 3 minutes. Cool in the pan.

Transfer the crusts to a cooling rack. Place the cheese and vanilla extract in a mixing bowl. Sift in the confectioners' sugar, then beat with a wooden spoon until smooth.

Place the strawberries on a cutting board. Remove the green stalks from the strawberries. Use a knife to cut them in half or quarters, if they are large.

When the crusts are completely cool, use a teaspoon to fill them with the mascarpone and vanilla mixture. Arrange the strawberries on top.

Place the red currant jelly in a small pan with the water and cook over low heat, stirring until the jelly has dissolved. Brush this over the strawberries.

Four ways with cookies

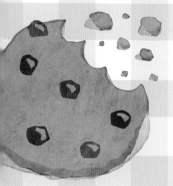

Everyone enjoys making cookies and everyone loves to eat them. Try these tasty combinations or come up with your own.

Basic cookie dough

This recipe is for 8 people (allowing for 2 cookies each). It takes 40 minutes to prepare and 15 minutes to cook.

- 7 tbsp butter, at room temperature
- 1 egg
- $2/3$ cup granulated sugar
- $1/2$ tsp pure vanilla extract
- $1\frac{1}{4}$ cups self-rising flour

Equipment

- 2 baking sheets
- parchment paper
- large glass bowl
- electric mixer
- wooden spoon

1

Hazelnut delights

Hazelnuts have a wonderful flavor and crunch. Alternatively, you can use the same quantity of another nut. Do you like peanuts, walnuts, pecans, or pistachios?

Ingredients

(to add to the basic dough recipe above)
- $2\frac{1}{2}$ oz (75g) hazelnuts, cut in half

Top tips

- Toast the nuts under the broiler for 2 minutes before you stir them into the dough mixture.
- Wrap up a stack of cookies in parchment paper and tie it with ribbon to make a gift for someone.

2

Cranberry chews

You can play around with tastes by adding different dried fruits to the cookie dough. Which is your favorite? Try raisins, mangoes, apples, blueberries, and cherries.

Ingredients

(to add to the basic dough recipe above)
- $1\frac{1}{2}$oz (45g) white chocolate, broken into small pieces
- $1/3$ cup dried cranberries, finely chopped

Top tips

- Mix the ingredients really well so that the cranberries and white chocolate don't all sit together. They need to be spread out in each cookie.
- Serve the cookies with a glass of milk for each person.

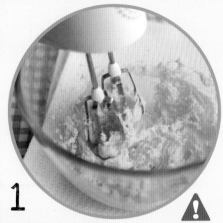

1

Preheat the oven to 350°F (180°C). Line two baking sheets with parchment paper. In a large bowl, use an electric mixer to beat the butter and egg together. Mix in the sugar and vanilla.

2

Work in the flour with a spoon until the mixture forms a soft dough, then mix in your additional ingredients from one of the recipes below. Chill in the refrigerator for 30 minutes.

3

Roll the dough into 16 balls and place on the baking sheets, leaving space around each ball. Flatten the balls slightly and bake in the oven for 15 minutes, or until golden. Cool them on a wire rack.

3

Traditional chocolate

This is a classic cookie that everyone likes. Why not try chunks of milk or white chocolate for a different taste twist? You can also mix it up by adding nuts to the recipe.

Ingredients

(to add to the basic dough recipe above)
- 2¹/₂oz (75g) dark chocolate, broken into small pieces

Top tips

- Make the chunks fairly big so that they are nice and gooey when you bite into a cookie.

- On a cold day, make hot chocolate to serve with the cookies for a real chocolatey treat.

4

Apricots and cinnamon

Other spices also work well instead of cinnamon. Add a quarter teaspoon of pumpkin pie spice or an eighth a teaspoon of ground ginger. Use raisins or golden raisins in place of apricots.

Ingredients

(to add to the basic dough recipe above)
- 2¹/₂oz (75g) dried apricots, finely chopped
- ¹/₄ tsp ground cinnamon

Top tips

- Chop the apricot pieces finely so that they are scattered well throughout each cookie.

- Store in a cookie tin for a few days, if they last that long!

Cupcakes

Whether you go for delicately or boldly decorated cupcakes, make sure you have enough toppings to choose from. Tie in with a theme if they're for a party.

Ingredients

- 11 tbsp unsalted butter, softened
- ¾ cup granulated sugar
- 1¼ cups self-rising flour
- 3 eggs, whisked
- ½ tsp pure vanilla extract

Icing and decoration

- 2¼ cups confectioners' sugar, sifted
- 2–3 tbsp hot water
- 3 different food colorings
- edible crystallized flowers, sugar strands, sprinkles, or candies

Equipment

- 2 x 12-hole muffin pans
- 20 baking cases
- 5 mixing bowls
- wooden spoon
- 2 metal spoons
- cooling rack
- strainer
- knife

1

Line 2 muffin pans with 20 baking cases—there are plenty of designs to choose from. Ask an adult to preheat the oven to 350°F (180°C).

2

Place the butter, sugar, self-rising flour, eggs, and vanilla extract in a bowl and beat with a wooden spoon until the mixture is pale in color and creamy.

3

Divide between the baking cases. Bake for 15 minutes, until golden and just firm. Cool in the pan for 5 minutes, then transfer to a wire rack to cool fully.

4

Trim any pointed tops to make a flat surface—this way, the icing will sit better, ready for your decorations.

Makes 20   30 mins   15 mins

5

Mix the confectioners' sugar in a large bowl and gradually stir in enough water to create a smooth, thick icing that coats the back of a spoon.

6

Transfer the icing mixture to 3 individual bowls and add a few drops of food coloring to each. Spoon onto the cupcakes and top with decorations. Allow to set.

Sponge cake

The easiest but still the most delicious cake, sponge cake can be made in the traditional way or zested up with some zingy lemon.

Serves 8   10 mins   30 mins

Grease the cake pans so that the cake doesn't stick. Ask an adult to preheat the oven to 350°F (180°C).

Place the butter, sugar, eggs, and vanilla extract in a large bowl and sift the flour and baking powder over the top. Using a handheld electric mixer or whisk, beat the ingredients together until thick.

Divide the mixture between the 2 pans, leveling the tops with the back of a tablespoon. Bake in the center of the oven for 25–30 minutes, or until risen and firm to the touch.

Leave the cakes to cool in the pans for 5–10 minutes, then turn them onto a cooling rack to allow them to cool completely.

To make the filling, place the butter, confectioners' sugar, vanilla extract, and milk in a mixing bowl. Beat them together with a wooden spoon until smooth and creamy.

Use a spatula to spread jam on the flat side of one of the cakes and put on a cake stand. Spread the flat side of the other with the frosting and put it on top. Finish with a dusting of confectioners' sugar.

Ingredients

- 12 tbsp butter, softened
- ⅞ cup granulated sugar
- 3 eggs, beaten
- 1 tsp pure vanilla extract
- 1½ cups self-rising flour
- 1 tsp baking powder

- ¼ cup raspberry or strawberry jam
- confectioners' sugar, for dusting

For the frosting

- 4 tbsp butter, softened
- 1 cup confectioners' sugar

- ½ tsp pure vanilla extract
- 2 tsp milk

Equipment

- 2 x 8in (20cm) round cake pans
- parchment paper
- large mixing bowl

- strainer
- electric mixer or whisk
- tablespoon
- oven mitts
- cooling rack
- mixing bowl
- wooden spoon
- spatula

Makes 15 15 mins 10 mins

Ingredients

- 2³/₄ cups all-purpose flour
- 2 tsp ground ginger
- 1 tsp baking soda
- 9 tbsp butter, cubed
- 1 cup dark brown sugar
- ¹/₄ cup corn syrup
- 1 egg, beaten
- candies, raisins, and icing, for decoration

Equipment

- 2 large baking sheets
- parchment paper
- large mixing bowl
- wooden spoon
- rolling pin
- cookie cutters of your choice
- oven mitts

Gingerbread

Fill your house with the wonderful smell

of baking gingerbread. Use unusual cookie cutters to make your shapes so your cookies will stand out from the crowd.

1

Ask an adult to preheat the oven to 350°F (180°C). Line 2 large baking sheets with parchment paper. If you only have 1 tray, you will need to bake the cookies in batches.

2

Place the flour, ginger, and baking soda in a large bowl. Stir the ingredients together with a wooden spoon until they are thoroughly mixed.

3

Rub the butter into the mixture using your fingertips. Continue rubbing in the butter until the mixture resembles fine bread crumbs. Stir in the sugar.

4

Stir in the corn syrup and egg until the mixture starts to come together in a dough. Next, turn the dough mixture onto a lightly floured surface and knead it until smooth.

5

Roll out the dough on a lightly floured surface to a thickness of ¼in (5mm). Using your cookie cutters, cut out the shapes. Re-roll the leftover dough and cut out more cookies until it's all used.

6

Place the cookies on the baking sheets and bake in the preheated oven for 9–10 minutes, or until golden. Allow the cookies to cool on the sheets. Decorate with candies, raisins, and icing.

Brownie

A real crowd-pleasi~~ng~~
brownies taste divine, wheth
made with white, milk, or da
If you want to serve big portio
into large pieces for all your gu

Ingredients

- 3oz (90g) dark chocolate
- 11 tbsp unsalted butter, diced, plus extra for greasing
- 1 cup all-purpose flour
- 3 tbsp cocoa powder
- ½ tsp baking powder
- pinch of salt
- 2 eggs
- 2 cups light brown sugar
- 1 tsp pure vanilla extract
- 4oz (100g) pecan nuts, chopped (optional)

Equipment

- 8in x 6in (20cm x 15cm) baking pan
- scissors
- pencil
- parchment paper
- 3 medium-sized bowls
- wooden spoon
- small saucepan
- strainer
- spatula
- palette knife
- oven mitts

1

Grease and line the bottom of the baking pan with parchment paper (see instructions on page 11). Ask an adult to preheat the oven to 350°F (180°C).

2

Break the chocolate into a bowl and add the chunks of butter. Melt the butter and chocolate over a saucepan of barely simmering water, stirring occasionally.

3

Remove the bowl from the heat and allow the chocolate to cool slightly. In a separate bowl, sift the flour, cocoa powder, baking powder, and salt.

4

In a third bowl, beat the eggs and then in add the sugar and vanilla extract. Stir the ingredients together until they are just mixed.

5

Fold the melted chocolate into the beaten egg mixture using a spatula. Then gently fold in the flour mixture and nuts, if using. You shouldn't be able to see any flour once it's all combined.

6

Spoon the mixture into the pan, smooth the top with a palette knife, and bake for 25 minutes. Allow the brownies to cool in the pan before cutting them into squares.

107

Ingredients

- 1¼ cups all-purpose flour
- 2 tsp baking powder
- ½ tsp baking soda
- ⅔ cup light brown sugar
- 2oz (50g) roasted hazelnuts, chopped
- 1 cup grated carrots
- 3½oz (100g) dried apricots, finely chopped
- 1 tbsp poppy seeds
- ½ tsp ground cinnamon
- ⅔ cup oats
- zest of 2 oranges
- 1 cup buttermilk, or 1 cup milk and 1 tbsp lemon juice
- 1 egg, beaten
- 3 tbsp melted butter
- pinch of salt
- juice of 1 large orange

For the topping

- 2 tbsp brown sugar
- ⅓ cup oats
- 1 tbsp melted butter

Equipment

- small glass bowl
- baking sheet
- cutting board
- sharp knife
- large glass bowl
- spoon
- baking cups
- muffin pan

Carrot and orange muffins

The versatile carrot can be savory or sweet, as in these delicious muffins—a perfect snack or lunchbox treat.

1

Ask an adult to preheat the oven to 400°F (200°C). To make the topping, mix together the ingredients in a bowl. Sprinkle the mixture onto a baking sheet. Bake for 5 minutes, then let cool.

2

In a large bowl, mix the flour, baking powder, baking soda, and sugar. Add the nuts, carrots, apricots, poppy seeds, cinnamon, oats, and orange zest. Mix together well.

3

In another bowl, use a spoon to mix the buttermilk, egg, butter, salt, and orange juice. Pour this liquid mixture onto the bowl of dry ingredients.

4

Stir the two mixtures together using a spoon. Be careful not to overmix, since this will "knock out" all the air. In fact, the lumpier the mixture, the better the muffins will be!

Makes 8   20 mins   25 mins

Flavor tryouts

For extra zing, use lemons instead of oranges. Or make a hole with your finger (after step 5) and add a chunk of white chocolate for a tasty, gooey center.

5

Place 8 baking cups in a muffin pan. Spoon the mixture into the baking cups, filling them two-thirds full.

6

Sprinkle the crumbly topping over the muffins. Bake in the preheated oven for 25–30 minutes, until well risen and golden. Let cool.

Extra recipe idea

Try out this recipe with 10oz (300g) of your favorite ingredients, such as bananas, strawberries, meringues, raspberries, or a chopped-up bar of chocolate.

Frozen yogurt

Create your new favorite icy alternative to ice cream by experimenting with flavors. You'll make enough for plenty of friends to cool down on a hot summer's day!

8-12 scoops   4 hrs 20 mins

Carefully chop the fudge and honeycomb (if using) into tiny pieces on a cutting board, then break up the cookies into slightly larger pieces.

Pour the cream into a mixing bowl and sift in the confectioners' sugar. Lightly whip the cream into soft peaks. (You can use a handheld electric mixer or a whisk.)

Gently fold the yogurt, honeycomb, fudge, cookies, and marshmallow pieces into the cream mixture using a plastic spatula or a metal spoon.

Spoon the mixture into the tubs, cover, and freeze. After 2 hours in the freezer, stir the mixture to prevent ice crystals from forming and then freeze for at least 2 hours more. It will then be ready to serve. If it thaws, do not refreeze.

Ingredients
- 3oz (85g) fudge
- 2oz (60g) honeycomb, optional
- 3oz (85g) chocolate chip cookies
- ⅔ cup heavy cream
- ¼ cup confectioners' sugar
- 2½ cups natural yogurt
- 1¼ cups mini marshmallows

Equipment
- cutting board
- sharp knife
- mixing bowl
- strainer
- whisk
- spatula or metal spoon
- 2 plastic tubs with lids

111

Mint chocolate pots

These luxurious, grown-up desserts are super-chocolatey, but with a minty kick. Dress them up with a stenciled shape of confectioners' sugar or cocoa.

Ingredients

- 1¼ cups heavy cream
- small bunch of mint, chopped
- ½ cup milk
- 6oz (175g) dark chocolate, broken into small pieces
- 3 egg yolks
- 1 tbsp confectioners' sugar, plus extra for dusting
- cocoa powder, for dusting (optional)

Equipment

- cutting board
- sharp knife
- 2 saucepans
- mixing bowl
- wooden spoon
- whisk
- strainer
- roasting pan
- 4 ramekins
- cardboard, pencil, scissors

Ask an adult to preheat the oven to 300°F (150°C). Pour the cream into a small pan and add the mint. Heat gently until nearly boiling, then remove from the heat, cover, and let stand for 30 minutes.

Meanwhile, pour the milk into another small pan and heat gently. Remove from the heat and stir in the chocolate pieces until melted and the mixture is smooth.

Whisk the egg yolks and sugar together and add the chocolatey milk and minty cream. Mix well, then strain the mixture through a fine strainer to remove the mint.

Pour the mixture into 4 ramekins that are standing in a roasting pan. Add hot water until it is halfway up the outside of the cups. Bake for 45–60 minutes. Let cool, then refrigerate for a few hours. Decorate just before serving, if you like.

Serves 4

45 mins

45-60 mins

Stencils

Make a stencil out of cardboard—stars, circles, and flowers work well—and sift some confectioners' sugar or cocoa powder on top for a knockout decoration.

Fridge cake

A no-bake cake! What could be easier? Plus, you get to smash some cookies. This cake uses nuts, but you can substitute different types of dried fruit, such as cranberries, for the nuts, if you like.

Ingredients

- 1lb (450g) graham crackers
- 11 tbsp butter
- 1lb 2oz (500g) dark chocolate, broken into pieces
- 2 tbsp corn syrup
- 1/3 cup raisins
- 2oz (50g) almonds, chopped

Equipment

- rolling pin
- plastic bag
- mixing bowl
- saucepan
- wooden spoon
- 7in x 7in (18cm x 18cm) baking pan
- parchment paper
- potato masher
- sharp knife
- cutting board

Place the crackers in a plastic bag and smash them with a rolling pin. Don't break them too finely, though. You need chunks, not dust.

Melt the butter, chocolate, and syrup in a bowl over a saucepan of hot water. Stir together to make a shiny mixture. Remove from the heat.

When the bowl is cool to the touch, stir in the crackers, raisins, and almonds. Make sure all the ingredients are mixed really well. Next, line the pan with parchment paper.

Use a potato masher to press the mixture into the pan and put it in the refrigerator to harden. Cut into 24 pieces. If you like, freeze some in an airtight container and eat within a few months.

Makes 24 · 10 mins · 1 hour

With a twist

For a crackly surprise, add 1¾oz (50g) popping candy after step 3. Don't open the packages until you need the candy or all the "popping-ness" will be lost.

Meringue crowns

These beautiful desserts look so impressive. The good news is that they are easier to make than they seem! Each crown is large and serves 2 people, so invite your friends around to share in the sweetness.

Serves 6   45 mins   2 hours

For the meringue
- 3 eggs
- 1 cup granulated sugar
- pinch of salt

For the filling
- ⅔ cup heavy cream, whipped (optional)
- 1 nectarine
- 1 mango
- 1 kiwi

Equipment
- baking sheet
- parchment paper
- large bowl
- electric mixer
- tablespoon
- metal mixing spoon
- piping bag
- oven mitts
- cutting board
- sharp knife
- large mixing bowl

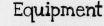

1

Line a baking sheet with parchment paper and ask an adult to preheat the oven to 225°F (110°C). Separate the egg whites from the yolks.

2

Whisk the egg whites and salt in a large bowl (using an electric mixer is easiest), until they form stiff peaks.

Berry-tastic
You can put any type of fruit into the meringue's center. Try a berry medley of blueberries, raspberries, and strawberries.

3

When the egg whites are stiff, whisk 5 tablespoons of the measured sugar into the mixture, 1 tablespoon at a time. Then, fold the remaining sugar into the mixture, using a metal spoon.

4

Draw 3 circles of 4in (10cm) diameter (a saucer works well) onto the parchment. Using a piping bag, squeeze out the mixture in a spiral. Pipe small peaks to create a crown. Three meringues fit on a sheet.

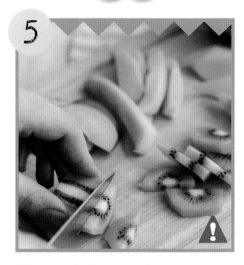

5

Toward the end of the meringue's baking time (on the bottom shelf for 2 hours), whip the cream until firm (if using) and carefully slice your fruit. Fill the center of each crown.

117

Berry
alternative

If blueberries aren't your
favorite, use blackberries
or raspberries instead.
Whichever you choose,
the end result will
be a knockout.

Blueberry cheesecake

Serves 4   10 mins   1 hr 20 mins

These layered desserts look impressive but are easy to make. If you make them in glasses, all your guests will be able to see the colorful layers.

1

Place three-quarters of the berries and half the sugar into a small saucepan. Cover and simmer for 5 minutes, until soft. Stir in the remaining berries and let cool.

2

Using a clean wooden spoon, beat the cream cheese, crème fraîche, remaining sugar, and vanilla extract together in a mixing bowl. Continue stirring until well mixed and soft.

3

Create a layered look by filling 4 glasses with a spoonful of the blueberry sauce, then a spoonful of the cream cheese mixture, and then a spoonful of the crushed cookies.

4

Repeat the layers once more and put the filled glasses in the refrigerator for an hour to give the mixture time to set. Serve chilled right from the fridge.

Ingredients
- 1lb 2oz (500g) blueberries
- 2 tbsp granulated sugar
- 8oz (250g) cream cheese
- 1 cup crème fraîche
- ¼ tbsp pure vanilla extract
- 8 oat cookies, crushed

Equipment
- small saucepan
- wooden spoon
- bowl
- tablespoon
- 4 glasses

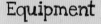

119

Oat crumble

A fruit crumble is a hearty dessert that will warm you up on a cold day. Apples are used in a traditional crumble, but you can also make it with pears or blackberries.

1

Preheat the oven to 350°F (180°C). For the topping, put the whole wheat and all-purpose flour into a large mixing bowl and stir together with a spoon.

2

Add the butter. Rub the butter and flour together with your fingertips until they look like coarse bread crumbs. Stir in the sugar, seeds, and oats, and set aside.

3

To make the filling, peel the apples and cut them into quarters. Carefully remove the core and slice the fruit into bite-sized pieces.

4

Put the pieces of apple into the dish. Add the blueberries and pour the apple juice over the top. Sprinkle with sugar.

5

Spoon over the topping in an even layer, then put the dish in the oven. Cook for 35 minutes, until the top is crisp and beginning to brown.

Variation

This works as a summer dessert, too. Try it with nectarines, peaches, plums, rhubarb, or raspberries. They're all great. Serve the dish with ice cream to make it extra summery.

Serves 6-8   25 mins   35 mins

Ingredients

For the topping

- ²/₃ cup all-purpose flour
- ²/₃ cup whole wheat flour
- 5 tbsp unsalted butter, cut into small pieces
- ½ cup light brown sugar
- 3 tbsp sunflower seeds
- 1 tbsp sesame seeds
- 3 tbsp oats

For the filling

- 4 sweet apples
- 7oz (200g) blueberries, defrosted (if frozen)
- ¼ cup fresh apple juice
- 1 tbsp light brown sugar

Equipment

- large mixing bowl
- small sharp knife
- cutting board
- 1-quart ovenproof dish
- small liquid measuring cup

PLANNING A PARTY

Pizza pops page 43

Strawberry tarts page 96

Finger foods and mini versions of your favorites work best at parties—then you don't even need utensils. Here are some of our party bests.

A pop-up invitation

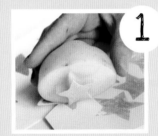

1 First, potato-print some stars onto construction paper. Once the prints are dry, cut them out, leaving a border around the edge.

2 Fold a piece of long white card stock in half, and in half again. This will make make four equal panels when you unfold the paper (as above).

3 Make two parallel cuts across the center (see above). Wiggle your finger under this strip until it stands up from the card. Apply glue to the outer panels of the card and stick them down.

4 Glue your cutout printed shape on to the raised strip. Decorate before writing in the time and place of your party.

Treats to take home

Decorate gingerbread shapes and put them on sticks. Place in individual plastic bags for great party favors. Yum!

123

A THREE-COURSE MEAL

Show off your cooking skills by preparing a meal for your friends or family. Serve up an easy feast by choosing at least two dishes that can be made in advance. Plan your time to make sure you and your table will be ready for your dinner guests.

Design a place card

1 Potato-print your design (we chose strawberries) onto cards. Add extra details with a fine paintbrush if you like.

NOTE: The "seeds" were made by making small holes in the potato.

2 Fold some card stock in half, and add paper panels for the names. Glue on your motif. For the last step, write your guests' names on the cards.

Jack

The finishing touches

It's time to set the table. Alongside flowers and your handmade menu, use some pretty decorated plastic utensils. Paint a fork with acrylic paint, and, when it's dry, tie with ribbon and glue onto the menu.

Tonight

Appetizer
Bruschetta with tiny tomatoes and mozzarella

Entree
Beef pasta

Dess
Mint choc pots

tiny tomatoes bruchetta page 50

Crinkly edged paper on top looks great

Brighten up your table with multicolored straws and napkins.

Flowers—from the garden or florist—make a pretty addition to any table.

Mint chocolate pots page 112

Jack

Beef pasta page 56

PICNIC TIME

Never be short of ideas for eating outdoors—or even an indoor picnic if rain dampens your plans. Just pick and choose from recipes in the book.

Cupcakes page 100

Things to bring

- picnic blanket
- bottles of drinks
- plates, cups, and utensils
- paper napkins
- sunshine!

Make a paper flag

1 You'll need a pencil, construction paper, skewers, scissors, and glue. Fold the paper and draw a flag shape on the fold and cut it out.

2 Paint a design on to the flag. Cover the inside with glue, press firmly around the skewer, and leave to dry. Plant each flag proudly in your food.

Vegetable tart page 78

Potato salad page 64

Brownies page 106

Picnic salad page 26

Hummus and veggie sticks always go down well.

Italian bread page 34

BBQ chicken page 74

Use the flags to identify vegetarian recipes perhaps, or any that contain nuts.